CUPCAKES
& MUFFINS

OVER 100 EASY-TO-FOLLOW RECIPES • EACH RECIPE PHOTOGRAPHED

CUPCAKES & MUFFINS

OVER 100 EASY-TO-FOLLOW RECIPES • EACH RECIPE PHOTOGRAPHED

WELDON
OWEN

Published by Weldon Owen Pty Ltd
59–61 Victoria Street, McMahons Point
Sydney, NSW 2060, Australia
Copyright © 2011 Weldon Owen Pty Ltd

Managing Director Kay Scarlett
Publisher Corinne Roberts
Creative Director Sue Burk
Images Manager Trucie Henderson
Senior Vice President, International Sales Stuart Laurence
Sales Manager, North America Ellen Towell
Administration Manager, International Sales Kristine Ravn
Production Director Todd Rechner
Production and Prepress Controller Mike Crowton
Production Controller Lisa Conway
Production Coordinator Nathan Grice

Designer Chris Andrew
Editorial Director Laura Thomson
Editor Laurie Black
Editorial Assistant Natalie Ryan

ISBN: 978-1-74252-130-5

Printed by 1010 Printing
Manufactured in China

The paper used in the manufacture of this book is sourced
from wood grown in sustainable forests. It complies with the
Environmental Management System Standard ISO 14001:2004

A WELDON OWEN PRODUCTION

CONTENTS

CUPCAKES & MUFFINS

Little cakes are delightful, and this book is full of them, from gorgeous frosted cupcakes to wholesome muffins, mixed up in minutes and ready to eat, warm out of the oven, just 30 minutes later. There are little French cakes called financiers too, which might be the best no-fail cakes you have ever baked.

You'll find more than 100 recipes that are ideal for morning tea, afternoon tea, school lunches, and even dessert. There are recipes for holidays and special occasions, including hints and useful tips for decorating cupcakes. Beautiful photography and easy-to-follow instructions make this the ultimate guide to little cakes.

We take the mystery out of baking by telling you all the essentials, then giving clear, brief instructions in each recipe. You could make your first batch of cupcakes or muffins today!

CUPCAKE ESSENTIALS

The basics
The basic method for making most cupcakes is to:
- beat butter and sugar
- beat in eggs
- sift dry ingredients together
- fold dry and wet ingredients into the butter mixture
- spoon into pan and bake

There are two important tips
- beat the butter, sugar and eggs very well, to ensure that the final mixture is light and airy;
- use as few folding actions as possible, to keep the mixture light; but, make sure that everything is well combined.

Uniformity
When filling pans or paper liners, divide the mixture evenly so that each one is filled to the same level. This will give equal-sized cupcakes, and it will ensure that all of them cook evenly, in the same amount of time.

Testing, testing
Most cupcakes can be tested with a skewer to see if they are cooked properly. A wooden skewer inserted in the center of a cake should come out clean. If batter sticks to the skewer, the cupcakes are not yet cooked and must be returned to the oven.

Some cupcakes have gooey components such as melted chocolate that might stick to the skewer. In this case, press the center of the top of a cupcake and see if the surface springs back once released. If the texture feels squishy, and the center does not spring back, cook the cupcakes a little longer.

Occasionally, recipes call for a fudgey texture. These cupcakes should feel squishy and should not be cooked any further, or they will dry out.

Know your pans
Cupcakes and muffins are made in the same pans.
- standard 12 x 1/3 cup (80ml) round recesses
- Texas 6 x 1 cup (250ml) round recesses
- mini 12 x 2 Tbsp (30ml) round recesses

Each recess should be greased, or lined with a paper liner of the correct size.

For greasing, use butter or a suitable spread, or use a light oil (spray or liquid). Take care to grease the whole surface of each recess, but grease sparingly.

Successful removals
Cupcakes in paper liners are simple to remove from the pan, but do leave them for a few minutes after they come out of the oven, while they are particularly delicate and likely to break if moved.

To remove cupcakes from a greased pan, cool for 5 to 10 minutes first, then ease each one from the pan in the following way:
- pull the edge away from the sides of pan
- gently twist the cupcake, easing it from the bottom of pan
- if necessary, use a butter knife to ease away any sticky bits

Saving for later
Freeze your cupcakes, unfrosted, for up to 6 weeks. Defrost in the refrigerator or at room temperature before frosting.

CUPCAKES

PECAN & COCONUT CHOCOLATE CUPCAKES

Makes 12

1 1/2 cups (190g) all-purpose (plain) flour

1 tsp baking powder

1/2 cup (110g) light brown (soft brown) sugar

1/3 cup (30g) unsweetened shredded (desiccated) coconut

1/4 cup (35g) chopped pecans

1 stick (125g) butter, melted

3 1/2 oz (100g) milk chocolate, melted

2 eggs, lightly beaten

1/4 cup (60g) sour cream

1/4 cup (60ml) milk

1 Tbsp grated milk chocolate, for decorating

Chocolate butter cream

6 Tbsp (90g) butter, softened

3/4 cup (115g) confectioners' (icing) sugar

3 Tbsp unsweetened cocoa powder

1 Tbsp milk

Preheat oven to 350ºF (180ºC). Lightly grease a standard muffin pan.

Sift flour and baking powder into a large bowl. Stir in sugar, coconut and pecans. Make a well in the center.

Stir in butter, chocolate, eggs, sour cream and milk. Mix well and spoon evenly into muffin pan.

Bake for 15 to 20 minutes, until a skewer inserted in the center of a cupcake tests clean. Cool in pan for 5 minutes, then transfer to a wire rack to cool completely.

To make chocolate butter cream, beat butter using electric mixer, until creamy. Sift the confectioners' sugar and cocoa powder together, and beat slowly into butter with milk, until well mixed. Spread over cooled cupcakes. Sprinkle grated chocolate on top.

RASPBERRY CHOCOLATE CUPCAKES

Makes 12

4 ½ oz (125g) semisweet (plain) chocolate, chopped

½ cup (125ml) milk

¼ cup (30g) unsweetened cocoa powder, sifted

1 stick (125g) butter, softened

½ cup (110g) superfine (caster) sugar

2 eggs

1 cup (125g) all-purpose (plain) flour

1 tsp baking powder

1 punnet fresh raspberries, for decorating

whipped cream, for serving

Chocolate glaze

14oz (400g) semisweet (plain) chocolate, chopped

½ cup (125ml) double (heavy) cream

1 Tbsp hazelnut-flavored liqueur (or use sweet sherry)

Preheat oven to 325°F (160°C). Grease a standard muffin pan.

Place chocolate, milk and cocoa powder in a small saucepan. Stir over a low heat, without boiling, until chocolate has melted and mixture is smooth. Remove from heat and allow to cool.

Using an electric mixer, beat butter and sugar until fluffy. Add eggs, one at a time, beating until combined. Sift flour and baking powder into a small bowl. Add flour and chocolate mixtures to butter mixture, stirring to combine.

Spoon mixture into prepared pan. Bake for about 25 minutes, or until a skewer inserted in the center of a cupcake tests clean. Set pan on a wire rack to cool.

To make chocolate glaze, place chocolate, cream and liqueur in a small heatproof bowl over a pan of simmering water. Stir until chocolate has melted.

Spread glaze over tops of cooled cupcakes. When ready to serve, decorate with raspberries. Serve with whipped cream.

APPLE CUPCAKES WITH STREUSEL TOPPING

Makes 12

1 stick (125g) butter, softened

²/₃ cup (150g) superfine (caster) sugar

1 tsp vanilla extract

2 eggs

2 cups (250g) all-purpose (plain) flour

2 tsp baking powder

²/₃ cup (160ml) milk

1 green apple, peeled, cored and finely chopped

Streusel topping

¼ cup (35g) all-purpose (plain) flour

3 Tbsp light brown (soft brown) sugar

1 tsp ground cinnamon

2 Tbsp (30g) butter, softened

¹/₃ cup (45g) chopped pecans

Preheat oven to 350ºF (180ºC). Line a standard muffin pan with paper cupcake liners.

Using electric mixer, beat butter and sugar together until fluffy. Beat in vanilla extract. Add eggs, one at a time, beating well after each addition.

Sift flour and baking powder into a small bowl. Fold flour mixture into butter mixture alternately with milk, beginning and ending with flour. Fold in apple. Spoon mixture into prepared liners to two-thirds full.

To make streusel topping, whisk together flour, sugar and cinnamon. Using fingertips, rub in butter. Stir in pecans. Sprinkle topping evenly over cupcakes.

Bake for 20 to 25 minutes, until a skewer inserted in the center of a cupcake tests clean. Cool in pan for 5 minutes, then transfer cupcakes to a wire rack to cool completely.

TIRAMISÙ CUPCAKES

Makes 6

1 stick (125g) butter, softened

⅔ cup (150g) superfine (caster) sugar

2 eggs, separated

1 tsp hazelnut-flavored liqueur

½ tsp vanilla extract

1 cup (120g) hazelnut meal

½ cup (65g) all-purpose (plain) flour

½ tsp baking powder

½ cup (125ml) milk

unsweetened cocoa powder, for dusting

chocolate hearts, for decorating (see note)

Coffee cream

½ cup (125ml) double (heavy) cream, whipped

1 tsp instant coffee powder (or finely crushed granules)

1 tsp confectioners' (icing) sugar

½ cup (115g) mascarpone

Preheat oven to 350°F (180°C). Line a Texas muffin pan with jumbo paper liners.

Using electric mixer, beat butter and sugar together until fluffy. Add egg yolks, one at a time, beating well after each addition. Beat in hazelnut liqueur and vanilla.

Whisk together hazelnut meal, flour and baking powder in a bowl.

On low speed, alternately add flour mixture and milk to butter mixture, beginning and ending with flour mixture.

In a clean bowl, beat egg whites until stiff peaks form. Lightly fold into the hazelnut mixture.

Spoon mixture into paper liners to two-thirds full. Bake for 30 to 35 minutes, or until a skewer inserted in the center of a cupcake tests clean.

Cool cupcakes in pan for 5 minutes, then transfer to a wire rack to cool completely.

To make coffee cream, gently fold whipped cream, coffee and sugar into mascarpone.

Using a sharp pointed knife, cut a circle from the top of each cake (the circles are not required). Fill cavities with coffee cream. Dust with cocoa powder and top with a chocolate heart.

Cupcake note Use melted chocolate and your choice of molds to make chocolate hearts or other shapes.

DOUBLE VANILLA CUPCAKES

Makes 12

½ stick (65g) butter, softened

1 cup (225g) sugar

1 tsp vanilla extract

2 eggs

1¼ cups (160g) + 2 Tbsp all-purpose (plain) flour

¾ tsp baking powder

½ cup (125ml) milk

small decorations of your choice, for sprinkling

Vanilla frosting

4 Tbsp (60g) butter, softened

2 cups (300g) confectioners' (icing) sugar, sifted

2 tsp vanilla extract

2 Tbsp milk

Preheat oven to 350°F (180°C). Line a standard muffin tin with paper cupcake liners.

Using electric mixer, beat butter, sugar and vanilla in a bowl until fluffy. Beat in eggs, one at a time.

Sift flour and baking powder together and add to butter mixture, alternating with milk, stirring to combine.

Spoon mixture into prepared liners to three-fourths full. Bake for 20 to 25 minutes, until a skewer inserted in the center of a cupcake tests clean. Transfer to a wire rack to cool.

To make vanilla frosting, whip all ingredients together in a bowl, then spread over cooled cupcakes. Sprinkle with decorations of your choice.

COCONUT MERINGUE CUPCAKES

Makes 24

2 sticks (250g) butter, softened

½ cup (110g) superfine (caster) sugar

3 egg yolks

1 cup (125g) all-purpose (plain) flour

1 tsp baking powder

½ cup (125ml) milk

½ tsp vanilla extract

Coconut meringue
3 egg whites

½ cup (110g) superfine (caster) sugar

1 cup (85g) unsweetened coconut flakes

Preheat oven to 350°F (180°C). Line two standard muffin pans with paper cupcake liners.

Using an electric mixer, beat the butter and sugar together until fluffy. Add the egg yolks, one at a time, beating well after each addition.

Sift the flour and baking powder into a small bowl. Fold the flour mixture into the butter mixture, alternating with the combined milk and vanilla.

Spoon the mixture into the prepared liners to half full. Bake for 20 minutes, until a skewer inserted in the center of a cupcake tests clean.

Meanwhile, to make coconut meringue, use a clean electric mixer and beat the egg whites until stiff peaks form. Gradually add the sugar, beating until thick and glossy. Use a metal spoon to gently fold in the coconut. Spread coconut meringue over the tops of the just-cooked cupcakes.

Bake cakes for a further 5 to 10 minutes, until meringue is just golden. Cool in the pans for 5 minutes, then transfer to a wire rack to cool completely.

HUMMINGBIRD CUPCAKES

Makes 12

1 cup (125g) all-purpose (plain) flour

1 tsp baking powder

¼ tsp baking soda (bicarbonate of soda)

1 tsp ground cinnamon

¾ cup (75g) unsweetened shredded (desiccated) coconut

¾ cup (95g) chopped pecans

⅔ cup (150g) dark brown (demerara) sugar

½ cup (125ml) vegetable oil

2 eggs, lightly beaten

¾ cup (170g) mashed ripe banana

¾ cup (185g) canned crushed pineapple

Frosting

4oz (100g) cream cheese, softened

2 Tbsp (30g) butter, softened

1 tsp finely grated lemon zest

1½ cups (225g) confectioners' (icing) sugar

Preheat oven to 350°F (180°C). Line a standard muffin pan with paper cupcake liners.

Sift flour, baking powder, baking soda and cinnamon together into a large bowl. Stir in coconut, pecans and sugar. Mix well.

Whisk together oil and eggs. Mix into flour mixture, stirring until smooth.

Add the banana and pineapple, stirring until well combined.

Spoon mixture into prepared liners. Bake for 25 to 30 minutes, until a skewer inserted in the center of a cupcake tests clean. Cool in pan for 5 minutes, then transfer to a wire rack to cool completely.

To make frosting, beat together the cream cheese, butter and lemon zest until light and fluffy. Slowly add sugar, beating until well combined. Spread over cooled cupcakes.

COFFEE CUPCAKES

Makes 12

1 stick (125g) butter, softened

⅔ cup (150g) light brown (soft brown) sugar

2 eggs

2 cups (250g) all-purpose (plain) flour

2 tsp baking powder

½ cup (120g) sour cream

½ cup (125ml) strong black coffee, cooled

12 pecans, for decorating

Coffee frosting

1 cup (150g) confectioners' (icing) sugar, sifted

1 Tbsp (15g) butter, melted

about 4 Tbsp hot strong black coffee

Preheat oven to 350°F (180°C). Line a standard muffin pan with paper cupcake liners.

Using electric mixer, beat butter and sugar together until fluffy. Add eggs one at a time, beating well after each addition.

Sift flour and baking powder into a small bowl. Whisk sour cream and coffee together. Fold flour mixture into butter mixture, alternating with sour cream and coffee, beginning and ending with flour.

Spoon mixture into prepared liners to two-thirds full. Bake for 20 to 25 minutes, until a skewer inserted in the center of a cupcake tests clean.

Cool in pan for 5 minutes, then transfer cupcakes to a wire rack to cool completely.

To make coffee frosting, combine confectioners' sugar and butter in a small heatproof bowl. Stir in just enough hot coffee to make a smooth paste. Place over a saucepan of simmering water and heat gently, stirring, for 2 to 3 minutes, until the mixture is spreadable. Spread over cooled cupcakes. Top with pecans.

MINI BANANA PASSIONFRUIT CAKES

Makes 24

½ stick (65g) butter, softened

¼ cup (55g) superfine (caster) sugar

1 tsp vanilla extract

1 egg

2 ripe bananas, mashed

½ tsp baking soda (bicarbonate of soda)

¼ cup (60ml) warm milk

1 cup (125g) all-purpose (plain) flour, sifted

1 tsp baking powder

¼ tsp ground nutmeg

Passionfruit frosting

1½ cups (225g) confectioners' (icing) sugar, sifted

2 Tbsp (30g) butter, melted

¼ cup (60g) fresh or canned passionfruit pulp

Preheat oven to 350°F (180°C). Grease two mini muffin pans.

Using an electric mixer, beat the butter and sugar in a bowl until fluffy.

Beat in the vanilla and egg, then beat in mashed banana. Combine baking soda with milk and beat into the mixture.

Sift together flour, baking powder and nutmeg and fold into the batter.

Spoon mixture into prepared pans. Bake for 15 to 20 minutes, until a skewer inserted in the center of a cupcake tests clean. Transfer to a wire rack to cool completely.

To make passionfruit frosting, combine all the ingredients in a bowl and beat until smooth. Spread over cooled cupcakes.

CHERRY & COCONUT CUPCAKES

Makes 14

1 stick (125g) butter, softened

1 cup (225g) superfine (caster) sugar

1 tsp vanilla extract

2 eggs

1/2 cup (45g) unsweetened fine desiccated coconut

1/2 cup (125ml) milk

1/2 cup (50g) fresh cherries, pitted and chopped

1 1/4 cups (160g) all-purpose (plain) flour

1 1/4 tsp baking powder

14 extra cherries, for decorating

Pink frosting

1 1/2 cups (225g) confectioners' (icing) sugar

juice of 1 lemon

few drops red food coloring

about 2 Tbsp boiling water

Heat oven to 375°F (190°C). Line two muffin pans with 14 paper cupcake liners.

Using an electric mixer, beat butter with sugar and vanilla until pale and creamy. Beat in eggs one at a time.

Stir in the coconut, then the milk and cherries. Sift in the flour and baking powder, stirring just enough to combine ingredients into a smooth batter.

Spoon mixture into prepared liners to three-fourths full. Bake for 20 to 25 minutes, until a skewer inserted in the center of a cupcake tests clean. Transfer pan to a wire rack to cool.

To make pink frosting, sift confectioners' sugar into a bowl. Stir in lemon juice and food coloring and just enough boiling water to form a smooth, pale pink frosting of pourable consistency.

Frost the cupcakes and decorate with fresh cherries.

SOUR CREAM MACADAMIA CRUMBLE CUPCAKES

Makes 12

1 stick (125g) butter, softened

½ cup (110g) light brown (soft brown) sugar

2 eggs

1 tsp vanilla extract

2 cups (250g) all-purpose (plain) flour

1 tsp baking powder

½ cup (120g) light sour cream

½ cup (125ml) milk

1 cup (125 g) chopped unsalted macadamias

Crumble topping

¾ cup (95g) chopped unsalted macadamias

⅓ cup (30g) old-fashioned rolled oats

3 Tbsp light brown (soft brown) sugar

4 tsp maple syrup

Preheat oven to 350°F (180°C). Line a standard muffin pan with paper cupcake liners.

Using an electric mixer, beat butter and sugar together until fluffy. Add eggs one at a time, beating well after each addition. Mix in vanilla.

Sift flour and baking powder into a small bowl. Combine sour cream. Fold flour mixture into butter mixture, alternating with combined sour cream and milk, and finishing with flour. Add macadamias and lightly fold through.

Spoon mixture into prepared liners.

To make crumble topping, place all ingredients in a bowl and stir to combine. Sprinkle evenly over each cupcake.

Bake cupcakes for 15 to 20 minutes, until a skewer inserted in the center of a cake tests clean.

Cool in pan for 5 minutes, then transfer cupcakes to a wire rack to cool completely.

BROWN SUGAR CUPCAKES WITH CHOCOLATE CANDY

Makes 12

1 stick (125g) butter, softened

²/₃ cup (150g) light brown (soft brown) sugar

1 tsp vanilla extract

2 eggs

1 ¾ cups (220g) all-purpose (plain) flour

2 tsp baking powder

²/₃ cup (160ml) milk

3oz (90g) readymade chocolate-coated malted milk ball candy

Chocolate frosting

1 ¾ cups (265g) confectioners' (icing) sugar

¼ cup (30g) unsweetened cocoa powder

1 Tbsp (15g) butter, melted

about 2 Tbsp boiling water

Preheat oven to 350°F (180°C) and line a standard muffin pan with paper cupcake liners.

Using electric mixer, cream butter and sugar until fluffy. Beat in the vanilla. Add eggs, one at a time, beating well after each addition.

Sift flour and baking powder into a small bowl. Fold flour mixture into butter mixture alternating with milk, beginning and ending with flour. Fold in half of the candy.

Spoon mixture into prepared liners to two-thirds full. Bake for 20 to 25 minutes, until a skewer inserted in the center of a cake tests clean.

Cool in pan for 5 minutes, then transfer cupcakes to a wire rack to cool completely.

To make chocolate frosting, sift confectioners' sugar and cocoa into a bowl. Beat in butter and enough water for a smooth, spreadable consistency. Spread over cooled cupcakes. Chop remaining candy and sprinkle over the frosted cupcakes, to decorate.

RASPBERRY & LEMON CUPCAKES WITH CREAM CHEESE FROSTING

Makes 12

1 stick (125g) butter, softened

²/₃ cup (150g) superfine (caster) sugar

1 tsp vanilla extract

2 eggs

2 cups (250g) all-purpose (plain) flour

2 tsp baking powder

¹/₂ cup (125ml) milk

¹/₂ cup (65g) fresh raspberries + 12 extra, for decorating

4 tsp confectioners' (icing) sugar

2 tsp finely grated lemon zest

Cream cheese frosting
9oz (250g) cream cheese, chopped, at room temperature

1¹/₂ cups (225g) confectioners' (icing) sugar

Preheat oven to 350°F (180°C). Line a standard muffin pan with paper cupcake liners.

Using electric mixer, beat butter and sugar together until fluffy. Beat in vanilla. Add the eggs one at a time, beating well after each addition.

Sift flour and baking powder into a small bowl. Fold flour mixture into butter mixture, alternating with milk, and beginning and ending with flour.

In another bowl, mash ¹/₂ cup (65g) raspberries and confectioners' sugar together, using a fork. Mix in zest. Fold raspberry pulp into the cake mixture.

Spoon into cases to two-thirds full. Bake for 20 to 25 minutes, until a skewer inserted in the center of a cupcake tests clean.

Cool in pan for 5 minutes, then transfer cupcakes to a wire rack to cool completely.

To make cream cheese frosting, beat cream cheese and confectioners' sugar together with electric mixer until smooth. Spread over cooled cupcakes. Top with raspberries.

PASSIONFRUIT CREAM BUTTERFLY CAKES

Makes 12

1 stick (125g) butter, softened

²/₃ cup (150g) superfine (caster) sugar

1 tsp vanilla extract

2 eggs

1 ¾ cups (220g) all-purpose (plain) flour

1 ¾ tsp baking powder

²/₃ cup (160ml) milk

confectioners' (icing) sugar, for dusting

Passionfruit cream

¾ cup (190ml) double (heavy) cream

¹/₃ cup (80ml) fresh or canned passionfruit pulp

Preheat oven to 350°F (180°C). Line a standard muffin pan with paper cupcake liners.

Using electric mixer, beat butter and sugar together until fluffy. Beat in vanilla, then the eggs, one at a time, beating well after each addition.

Sift flour and baking powder into a small bowl. Fold the flour mixture into butter mixture, alternating with milk, and beginning and ending with flour.

Spoon mixture into prepared liners. Bake for 20 to 25 minutes, until a skewer inserted in the center of a cupcake tests clean. Cool in pan for 5 minutes. Transfer cupcakes to a wire rack to cool completely.

To make passionfruit cream, whip cream to soft peaks. Gently fold passionfruit pulp into cream.

Using a sharp knife, cut a shallow circle about 1 ½ inches (4cm) in diameter from the top of each cupcake. Cut removed circles in half. Spoon passionfruit cream into each recess. Position cake tops in cream to form wings. Dust lightly with confectioners' sugar before serving.

COFFEE & BUTTERSCOTCH CUPCAKES

Makes 12

1 stick (125g) butter, softened

⅓ cup (75g) light brown (soft brown) sugar

¼ cup (60ml) light corn syrup

1 Tbsp light molasses

2 eggs

2 cups (250g) all-purpose (plain) flour

2 tsp baking powder

½ cup (120g) sour cream

½ cup (125ml) milk

candied macadamias or other candied nuts, chopped, for decorating

Coffee frosting

1 cup (150g) confectioners' (icing) sugar, sifted

1 Tbsp (15g) butter, melted

about 2 Tbsp hot, strong black coffee

Preheat oven to 350°F (180°C). Line a standard muffin pan with paper cupcake liners.

Using an electric mixer, beat butter, sugar, corn syrup and molasses together until fluffy. Add eggs one at a time, beating well after each addition.

Sift flour and baking powder into a small bowl. Stir sour cream and milk together. Fold flour mixture into butter mixture, alternating with combined sour cream and milk, and beginning and ending with flour.

Spoon the mixture into cases to two-thirds full. Bake for 20 to 25 minutes, until a skewer inserted in the center of a cupcake tests clean.

Cool in pan for 5 minutes, then transfer cupcakes to a wire rack to cool completely.

To make coffee frosting, combine confectioners' sugar and butter in a small bowl. Stir in enough coffee to make a smooth, spreadable paste. Frost cooled cakes. Top with chopped nuts.

SOUR CREAM BANANA CUPCAKES WITH CHOCOLATE FROSTING

Makes 18

1 stick (125g) butter, softened

¾ cup (170g) firmly packed light brown (soft brown) sugar

2 eggs, lightly beaten

1½ cups (190g) all-purpose (plain) flour

1½ tsp baking powder

1 tsp baking soda (bicarbonate of soda)

¾ cup (170g) mashed very ripe bananas

¾ cup (175g) sour cream

4 tsp milk

18 dried banana chips, for decorating

Milk chocolate ganache
9oz (250g) milk chocolate, finely chopped

½ cup (125ml) double (heavy) cream

Preheat oven to 350ºF (180ºC). Line 18 holes of two standard muffin pans with paper cupcake liners.

Using electric mixer, beat butter and sugar together until fluffy. Add eggs one at a time, beating well after each addition.

Sift flour, baking powder and baking soda over the creamed mixture. Fold in along with the banana, sour cream and the milk until combined.

Spoon mixture into prepared liners to two-thirds full. Bake for 20 to 25 minutes, until a skewer inserted in the center of a cupcake tests clean.

Cool in pan for 5 minutes, then transfer cupcakes to a wire rack to cool completely.

To make milk chocolate ganache, combine chocolate and cream in a medium saucepan. Stir over a low heat, until smooth. Cool to room temperature, to allow to thicken.

Spread ganache over cooled cupcakes. Top with banana chips.

LEMON CREAM CHEESE CUPCAKES

Makes 8

1 stick (125g) butter, softened

¾ cup (170g) sugar

1 Tbsp grated lemon zest

2 eggs

1 cup (125g) all-purpose (plain) flour

1 tsp baking powder

5oz (125g) cream cheese, cut into small cubes, softened

¼ cup (60ml) fresh lemon juice

Lemon curd frosting

¼ cup (85g) readymade lemon curd

1 Tbsp lemon juice

1¼ cups (190g) confectioners' (icing) sugar

Preheat oven to 400ºF (200ºC). Line eight holes in a standard muffin pan with paper cupcake liners.

Using an electric mixer, beat the butter, sugar and lemon zest together until fluffy. Add the eggs one at a time, beating well after each addition.

Sift flour and baking powder into butter mixture. Fold in with cream cheese and lemon juice, and mix just to combine.

Spoon mixture into prepared liners. Bake 12 to 15 minutes, until golden. Transfer to a wire rack to cool.

To make lemon curd frosting, whisk lemon curd, lemon juice and confectioners' sugar together until smooth. Spread over cooled cupcakes to serve.

NUTTY CARROT CUPCAKES | Gluten free

Makes 10

¹⁄₃ cup (55g) rice flour

¹⁄₃ cup (45g) cornstarch (cornflour)

2 Tbsp pumpkin pie spice (mixed spice)

2 tsp baking powder

1 tsp baking soda (bicarbonate of soda)

2 cups (240g) almond meal

1 cup (225g) firmly packed light brown (soft brown) sugar

2 carrots, peeled and grated

²⁄₃ cup (90g) walnuts, chopped

4 eggs, separated

Cream cheese frosting
9oz (250g) cream cheese, at room temperature

¹⁄₂ cup (75g) confectioners' (icing) sugar

1 Tbsp fresh orange juice

Preheat oven to 325°F (160°C). Line 10 holes of a standard muffin pan with paper cupcake liners.

Sift rice flour, cornstarch, pumpkin pie spice, baking powder and baking soda into a bowl. Stir in almond meal, sugar, carrot, half the walnuts and all the egg yolks; mix well.

Using electric mixer, in a large, clean bowl, beat egg whites until stiff peaks form. Lightly fold into almond and carrot mixture.

Spoon evenly into cases to two-thirds full. Bake for 20 to 25 minutes, until a skewer inserted in the center of a cupcake tests clean. Cool in pan for 5 minutes, then transfer to a wire rack to cool completely.

To make cream cheese frosting, beat cream cheese, sugar and orange juice, until well combined. Chill before using. Spread over cooled cupcakes. Sprinkle with remaining walnuts.

CHOCOLATE BERRY CUPCAKES WITH CREAM | Gluten free

Makes 16

1 cup (160g) rice flour

¾ cup (95g) cornstarch (cornflour)

⅓ cup (40g) unsweetened cocoa powder

1¼ tsp baking soda (bicarbonate of soda)

1 cup (225g) light brown (soft brown) sugar

1 cup (250ml) buttermilk

1 stick (125g) butter, melted

2 eggs

1½ cups (190g) fresh or frozen raspberries

¾ cup (190ml) double (heavy) cream, whipped, for serving

extra unsweetened cocoa powder, for serving

Preheat oven to 350°F (180°C). Line 16 holes of two standard muffin pan with paper cupcake liners.

Sift rice flour, cornstarch, cocoa powder and baking soda together into a large bowl. Whisk in sugar.

Whisk together buttermilk, butter and eggs. Stir gently into dry ingredients. Add raspberries and mix lightly.

Spoon mixture evenly into prepared liners to two-thirds full. Bake for 20 to 25 minutes, until a skewer inserted in the center of a cupcake tests clean.

Cool in pan for 5 minutes, then transfer to a wire rack to cool completely.

When ready to serve, slice a small circle off the top of each cupcake. Pile whipped cream in indent, replace tops and dust with cocoa powder.

LEMON COCONUT CUPCAKES

Makes 24

1 stick (125g) butter, softened

¾ cup (170g) superfine (caster) sugar

2 eggs

1 tsp vanilla extract

1 cup (125g) all-purpose (plain) flour

1 tsp baking powder

½ cup (45g) unsweetened shredded (desiccated) coconut

½ cup (125ml) fresh lemon juice

unsweetened flaked coconut, toasted, for decorating

Lemon frosting

2 cups (300g) confectioners' (icing) sugar

1 Tbsp (15g) butter, melted

about 2 Tbsp fresh lemon juice

Preheat oven to 350ºF (180ºC). Lightly grease two standard muffin pans or line with paper cupcake liners.

Using an electric mixer, beat butter and sugar together in a large bowl until fluffy. Add eggs, one at a time, beating well after each addition. Mix in vanilla.

Sift flour and baking powder into a small bowl. Lightly fold flour mixture, coconut and lemon juice alternately into butter mixture, beginning and ending with flour.

Spoon mixture into prepared pans or liners to three-fourths full. Bake for 12 to 15 minutes, until a skewer inserted in the center of a cupcake tests clean.

Cool in pans for 5 minutes, then transfer cupcakes to a wire rack to cool completely.

To make lemon frosting, sift confectioners' sugar into a bowl. Beat in butter and lemon juice until smooth and spreadable. Spread over cooled cupcakes. Top with toasted coconut.

MINI RHUBARB CUPCAKES

Makes 24

4 Tbsp (60g) butter, softened

¼ cup (55g) light brown (soft brown) sugar

1 egg

½ tsp vanilla extract

1 cup (125g) all-purpose (plain) flour

1 tsp baking powder

½ cup (125ml) milk

½ cup (60g) finely chopped fresh rhubarb

2 tsp finely grated lemon zest

Preheat oven to 350°F (180°C). Line two mini muffin pans with mini paper cupcake liners.

Using electric mixer, beat butter and sugar together until fluffy. Add egg and vanilla, beating well.

Sift flour and baking powder into a small bowl. Fold in flour mixture alternately with milk. Gently stir in rhubarb and lemon zest.

Spoon mixture evenly into prepared liners. Bake for 12 to 15 minutes, until a skewer inserted in the center of a cupcake tests clean.

Cool in pans for 5 minutes, then transfer to a wire rack to cool completely.

TRIPLE CHOCOLATE MOCHA CUPCAKES

Makes 12

1 stick (125g) butter, chopped

1 cup (225g) superfine (caster) sugar

3½ oz (100g) semisweet (plain) chocolate, chopped

½ cup (125ml) hot water

3 Tbsp coffee liqueur

1 cup (125g) all-purpose (plain) flour

tiny pinch of baking powder

3 Tbsp unsweetened cocoa powder

1 egg, beaten

silver cachous, for decorating

White chocolate ganache
4oz (100g) white chocolate, chopped

3 Tbsp double (heavy) cream

Preheat oven to 350°F (180°C). Line a standard muffin pan with paper cupcake liners.

In a medium saucepan, combine butter, sugar, chocolate, water and liqueur. Stir over low heat until smooth. Transfer mixture to a medium bowl. Cool for 10 minutes.

Sift flour, baking powder and cocoa powder together. Fold into chocolate mixture. Stir in egg.

Spoon mixture into paper cases to two-thirds full. Bake for 20 to 25 minutes, until the center of a cake springs back when lightly pressed. Cool in pan for 5 minutes, then transfer to a wire rack to cool completely.

To make white chocolate ganache, combine chocolate and cream in a heatproof bowl. Heat over a saucepan of simmering water, stirring until melted. Using an electric mixer, beat chocolate mixture for 3 to 5 minutes, until thick and fluffy. Spread over cooled cupcakes. Decorate cupcakes with cachous.

GOLDEN RAISIN CUPCAKES WITH LEMON GLAZE

Makes 12

1 stick (125g) butter, softened

²/₃ cup (150g) superfine (caster) sugar

1 tsp vanilla extract

2 eggs

¾ cup (95g) all-purpose (plain) flour

¾ tsp baking powder

²/₃ cup (160ml) milk

¾ cup (110g) golden raisins (sultanas)

readymade sugar flowers, for decorating

Lemon glaze
2 cups (300g) confectioners' (icing) sugar

1 Tbsp (15g) butter, melted

about 2 Tbsp fresh lemon juice

Preheat oven to 350ºF (180ºC). Line a standard muffin pan with paper cupcake liners.

Using electric mixer, beat butter and sugar together until fluffy. Beat in the vanilla. Add eggs, one at a time, beating well after each addition.

Sift flour and baking powder into a small bowl. Fold flour mixture into butter mixture, alternating with the milk, and beginning and ending with flour. Fold in the raisins.

Spoon mixture into prepared liners to two-thirds full. Bake for 20 to 25 minutes, until a skewer inserted in the center of a cupcake tests clean. Cool in pan for 5 minutes. Transfer cupcakes to a wire rack to cool completely.

To make lemon glaze, sift sugar into a bowl. Beat in butter and enough lemon juice for a smooth consistency. Spread over cooled cupcakes. Decorate with sugar flowers.

ORANGE & COCONUT CUPCAKES

Makes 12

¼ cup (25g) unsweetened shredded (desiccated) coconut

2 Tbsp finely grated orange zest

¼ cup (60ml) fresh orange juice

1 stick (125g) butter, softened

¾ cup (170g) superfine (caster) sugar

2 eggs

1 cup (125g) all-purpose (plain) flour

1 tsp baking powder

¼ cup (35g) shelled natural pistachios, chopped

Orange frosting
2 Tbsp (30g) butter, melted

2 Tbsp fresh orange juice

2 cups (300g) confectioners' (icing) sugar

Preheat oven to 350°F (180°C). Line a standard muffin pan with paper cupcake liners.

Place coconut in a bowl. Add 1 tablespoon of the orange zest and all the juice and stir to combine.

Using an electric mixer, beat butter and sugar until fluffy. Add eggs, one at a time, mixing well after each addition.

Sift flour and baking powder over butter mixture. Add coconut orange mixture and fold ingredients together to combine.

Spoon mixture into liners. Bake for 12 to 15 minutes, until the center of a cake springs back when lightly pressed. Transfer to a wire rack to cool.

To make orange frosting, beat the butter, orange juice and confectioners' sugar together to make a firm mixture. Spread over the cooled cupcakes, and immediately sprinkle with chopped pistachios and remaining orange zest.

PLUM CRUMBLE CUPCAKES

Makes 6

1 ½ sticks (185g) butter, softened

¾ cup (170g) superfine (caster) sugar

2 tsp vanilla extract

3 eggs

1 ½ cups (190g) all-purpose (plain) flour

1 tsp baking powder

½ cup (60g) hazelnut meal

½ cup (125ml) milk

3 firm, ripe plums, halved, stones removed, thinly sliced

Crumble topping

⅓ cup (45g) all-purpose (plain) flour

4 Tbsp (60g) cold butter, finely chopped

½ cup (110g) dark brown (demerara) sugar

¼ cup (35g) coarsely chopped hazelnuts

Honey cream

¾ cup (190ml) whipped cream

2 tsp mild liquid honey

¼ tsp ground ginger

Preheat oven to 350ºF (180ºC). Line a Texas muffin pan with jumbo paper liners

Using electric mixer, beat butter, sugar and vanilla together until fluffy. Add eggs one at a time, beating well after each addition.

Whisk flour, baking powder and hazelnut meal together in a bowl. Fold flour mixture and milk into butter mixture, until just combined.

Spoon mixture in to prepared liners. Lightly press plum slices into batter.

To make crumble topping, sift flour into a small bowl. Rub butter into flour, using fingertips, until the mixture resembles fine breadcrumbs. Add half the sugar and all the hazelnuts. Sprinkle on top of cakes. Top each one with a little of the remaining sugar.

Bake for 30 to 35 minutes, until a skewer inserted in the center of a cupcake tests clean. Cool in pan for 5 minutes.

To make honey cream, fold all ingredients together gently in a small bowl. Serve warm cupcakes with honey cream.

CHOCOLATE SPICE CUPCAKES

Makes 12

1 stick (125g) butter, softened

1 cup (225g) firmly packed light brown (soft brown) sugar

2 eggs

1½ cups (190g) all-purpose (plain) flour

1½ tsp baking powder

1 tsp ground cinnamon

2 tsp pumpkin pie spice (mixed spice)

¼ cup (30g) unsweetened cocoa powder

¾ cup (190ml) milk

Simple chocolate frosting
1½ cups (225g) confectioners' (icing) sugar

2 Tbsp unsweetened cocoa powder

1 Tbsp (15g) butter, melted

3 Tbsp boiling water

Preheat oven to 350°F (180°C). Line a standard muffin pan with paper cupcake liners.

Using an electric mixer, beat the butter and sugar until fluffy. Add eggs and beat to combine.

Whisk together the flour, baking powder, spices and cocoa powder in another bowl, and add to the butter mixture in two batches alternating with the milk, mixing to form a smooth batter.

Spoon the mixture into prepared paper liners and bake for 25 minutes, or until a skewer inserted in the center of a cupcake tests clean. Transfer to a wire rack to cool.

To make simple chocolate frosting, sift confectioners' sugar and cocoa into a bowl. Add butter and boiling water and stir until smooth. Spread over cooled cupcakes.

COCONUT CUPCAKES

Makes 12

1 stick (125g) butter, softened

½ cup (110g) superfine (caster) sugar

1 tsp coconut extract

3 eggs

¾ cup (95g) all-purpose (plain) flour

¾ tsp baking powder

½ cup (45g) unsweetened shredded (desiccated) coconut

½ cup (45g) unsweetened fine desiccated coconut, for decorating

Coconut frosting
1 cup (150g) confectioners' (icing) sugar, sifted

½ tsp coconut extract

about 3 Tbsp milk

Heat oven to 350°F (180°C). Line a standard muffin pan with paper cupcake liners.

Using an electric mixer, beat together all the cake ingredients in a bowl, just enough to combine into a creamy batter.

Spoon mixture into prepared liners to three-fourths full. Bake for 20 minutes, until a skewer inserted in the center of a cupcake tests clean. Transfer to a wire rack to cool.

To make coconut frosting, whisk confectioners' sugar and coconut extract with enough milk to form a smooth mixture. Pour a spoonful over each cupcake and sprinkle with extra coconut, to decorate.

BANANA BUTTERMILK CUPCAKES

Makes 24

1 stick (125g) butter, softened

1 ½ cups (335g) superfine (caster) sugar

1 tsp vanilla extract

2 large ripe bananas, mashed

3 eggs

2 ½ cups (315g) all-purpose (plain) flour

1 tsp baking powder

1 tsp baking soda (bicarbonate of soda)

¾ cup (190ml) buttermilk

Frosting
5 Tbsp (75g) butter, softened

2 ½ cups (375g) confectioners' (icing) sugar, sifted

a few drops food colouring (optional)

about 2 Tbsp boiling water

Preheat oven to 350°F (180°C). Line two standard muffin pans with paper cupcake liners.

Using an electric mixer, beat butter, sugar and vanilla until pale and creamy.

Beat in mashed banana, then beat in eggs one at a time. Sift dry ingredients together and fold into mixture, alternating with the buttermilk. Stir just enough to combine to make a creamy batter.

Spoon mixture into prepared liners to three-fourths full. Bake for 20 to 25 minutes, until a skewer inserted in the center of a cupcake tests clean. Transfer to a wire rack to cool.

To make frosting, beat ingredients together, adding just enough boiling water to make a stiff and creamy mixture. Pipe frosting onto cooled cupcakes.

MINI ORANGE CUPCAKES

Makes 30

½ stick (65g) butter, softened

¼ cup (55g) superfine (caster) sugar

1 egg

½ tsp vanilla extract

1 cup (125g) all-purpose (plain) flour

1 tsp baking powder

⅓ cup (80ml) fresh orange juice

⅓ cup (80ml) natural vanilla yogurt

Frosting
½ cup (75g) confectioners' (icing) sugar

1 Tbsp fresh orange juice

Preheat oven to 350ºF (180ºC). Line 30 holes in three mini muffin pans with mini paper cupcake liners.

Using an electric mixer, beat butter and sugar together until fluffy. Add egg and vanilla, beating well.

Sift flour and baking powder into a small bowl. Fold flour mixture into butter mixture alternating with juice and yogurt.

Spoon mixture carefully into paper liners. Bake for 12 to 15 minutes, until a skewer inserted in the center of a cupcake tests clean. Transfer to a wire rack to cool.

To make frosting, beat ingredients together until smooth. Spread over cooled cupcakes.

GINGER PEAR CUPCAKES

Makes 12

1 stick (125g) butter, softened

½ cup (110g) light brown (soft brown) sugar

2 eggs

2 firm ripe pears

1½ cups (190g) all-purpose (plain) flour

1½ tsp baking powder

2 tsp ground ginger

½ cup (125ml) milk

extra 2 Tbsp light brown (soft brown) sugar, for topping

Preheat oven to 350°F (180°C). Line a standard muffin pan with paper cupcake liners.

Using an electric mixer, beat butter and ½ cup (110g) of light brown sugar until fluffy. Add eggs one at a time, beating well after each addition.

Peel pears and remove cores. Set aside half a pear and roughly chop the rest of the fruit. Mix the chopped pear into the butter and brown sugar. Sift flour, baking powder and ginger over the mixture and stir in gently with milk.

Spoon mixture into prepared liners.

Slice the remaining half pear and arrange slices on top of each cupcake. Sprinkle with the remaining brown sugar and bake for 15 minutes, until a skewer inserted into the center of a cupcake tests clean. Transfer to a wire rack to cool.

BLUEBERRY & HONEY CUPCAKES

Makes 10

1 ½ sticks (185g) butter, softened

½ cup (110g) superfine (caster) sugar

3 Tbsp liquid honey

1 tsp vanilla extract

3 eggs

1 ½ cups (190g) all-purpose (plain) flour

1 tsp baking powder

1 cup (125g) blueberries (fresh or frozen)

confectioners' (icing) sugar, for dusting

Preheat oven to 350°F (180°C). Line a standard muffin tin with 10 paper cupcake liners.

Using an electric mixer, beat butter, sugar, honey and vanilla until pale and creamy.

Beat in eggs one at a time. Sift dry ingredients together and stir into butter mixture just until combined. Stir in blueberries.

Spoon mixture into prepared liners to three-fourths full. Bake for 20 to 25 minutes, or until a skewer inserted in the center of a cupcake tests clean.

Transfer to a wire rack to cool. Dust the cupcakes with confectioners' sugar before serving.

CHOCOLATE JELLY CREAM CAKES

Makes 4

2oz (60g) semisweet (plain) chocolate, finely chopped

¼ cup (30g) unsweetened cocoa powder

½ cup (110g) firmly packed light brown (soft brown) sugar

¼ cup (60ml) boiling water

1 egg yolk

2 Tbsp almond meal

3 Tbsp all-purpose (plain) flour

2 egg whites

½ cup (125g) cream, whipped

⅓ cup (110g) jelly (jam), such as cherry, raspberry or strawberry

extra unsweetened cocoa powder, for dusting

Preheat oven to 350°F (180°C). Grease four holes only in a standard muffin pan.

Place chocolate, cocoa, sugar and water in a bowl and stir until smooth. Whisk in egg yolk, then stir in the almond meal and flour.

In a clean bowl, whisk the egg whites until glossy and white, and soft peaks form. Gently fold the egg whites into the chocolate mixture.

Spoon mixture into muffin pans. Bake for 25 to 30 minutes, until a skewer inserted in the center of a cupcake tests clean but moist.

Transfer cupcakes to a wire rack to cool. Just before serving, split cakes in half and sandwich them together with jelly and whipped cream. Dust tops with cocoa powder and serve.

FRUIT SALAD CUPCAKES

Makes 12

1 stick (125g) butter, softened

2/3 cup (150g) superfine (caster) sugar

1 tsp vanilla extract

2 eggs

2 cups (250g) all-purpose (plain) flour

2 tsp baking powder

2/3 cup (160ml) milk

1 green-skinned apple, peeled, cored and chopped

1 firm, ripe pear, peeled, cored and chopped

silver cachous, for decorating

Orange glaze

1 1/2 cups (225g) confectioners' (icing) sugar

3 Tbsp fresh orange juice

1 tsp soft butter

Preheat oven to 350°F (180°C). Line a standard muffin pan with paper cupcake liners.

Using electric mixer, beat butter and sugar together until fluffy. Beat in vanilla. Add eggs one at a time, beating well after each addition.

Sift flour and baking powder into a small bowl. Fold flour mixture into butter mixture, alternating with milk, and beginning and ending with flour. Fold in fruit.

Spoon mixture into paper cases to two-thirds full. Bake for 20 to 25 minutes, until a skewer inserted in the center of a cupcake tests clean.

Cool in pan for 5 minutes, then transfer to a wire rack to cool completely.

To make orange glaze, combine confectioners' sugar, orange juice and butter in a heatproof bowl. Place over a saucepan of simmering water. Stir until smooth. Spread over cooled cupcakes. Decorate with cachous.

SUGAR PLUM CUPCAKES

Makes 12

1 stick (125g) butter, softened

1 cup (225g) superfine (caster) sugar

2 large eggs

½ cup (115g) sour cream

finely grated zest of 1 orange

1 cup (125g) all-purpose (plain) flour

1 tsp baking powder

4 plums, stones removed, thinly sliced

⅓ cup (75g) raw (turbinado) sugar, for sprinkling

Preheat oven to 350°F (180°C). Lightly grease a standard muffin pan.

Using an electric mixer, beat butter and sugar in a bowl, until fluffy. Beat in eggs, sour cream and orange zest.

Sift flour and baking powder over the butter mixture and stir to combine.

Spoon mixture into prepared pan. Arrange a few slices of plum on the top of each cupcake. Sprinkle a little raw sugar on top of each one.

Bake for 25 to 30 minutes, until a skewer inserted in the center of a cupcake tests clean. Transfer to a wire rack to cool.

GINGER CHOCOLATE FUDGE MINI CUPCAKES

Makes 24

1 ¼ sticks (150g) butter, chopped

10 ½ oz (300g) semisweet (plain) chocolate, roughly chopped

3 large eggs

⅓ cup (75g) sugar

1 tsp vanilla extract

½ cup (80g) crystallized ginger, coarsely sliced

pinch of salt

½ cup (115g) mascarpone, for serving

Preheat oven to 350°F (180°C). Grease two mini muffin pans.

Place butter and chocolate in a heatproof bowl set over a saucepan of simmering water to melt (or microwave in short bursts on full power), stirring until smooth. Set aside to cool a little.

Using electric mixer, beat eggs, sugar, vanilla and salt in another bowl for 5 minutes, or until thick and pale. Gradually add melted chocolate mixture, continuing to beat, until well combined.

Spoon batter into prepared mini muffin pans and sprinkle surface of each with sliced ginger. Bake for 20 to 25 minutes, until a skewer inserted in the center of a cupcake tests sticky but the batter is not liquid.

Leave cupcakes to cool in tins for 10 minutes before running a small palette knife around the edges and carefully turning out. Serve warm or cold with a teaspoon of mascarpone on each.

Cupcake note These lovely, gooey fudge cakes are a little difficult to remove from the pans, due to the flourless nature of the mixture. As the cakes are very soft, any damage caused when removing them can easily be fixed by quickly pressing them back into shape.

CARAMEL NUT CHOCOLATE CUPCAKES

Makes 6

1 stick (125g) butter, softened

¾ cup (170g) light brown
(soft brown) sugar

2 eggs

1 cup (125g) all-purpose (plain) flour

1 tsp baking powder

2 Tbsp unsweetened cocoa powder

3½ oz (100g) milk chocolate, melted

⅔ cup (160ml) milk

whipped cream, for serving

Nut topping
4 Tbsp (60g) butter, chopped

¼ cup (55g) light brown
(soft brown) sugar

2 Tbsp pouring cream

¼ cup (35g) chopped unsalted
macadamias

¼ cup (35g) shelled natural
pistachios, chopped

¼ cup (35g) chopped unsalted
pecans

Preheat oven to 350°F (180°C). Lightly grease a Texas muffin pan.

First prepare nut topping. Combine butter, sugar and cream in a small saucepan. Stir over a low heat, without boiling, until sugar dissolves. Bring to a boil, then immediately remove from heat and stir in nuts. Spoon evenly into muffin pan. Freeze while making cupcakes.

Using an electric mixer, beat butter and sugar together until fluffy. Add eggs one at a time, beating well after each addition.

Whisk flour, baking powder and cocoa powder together in a bowl. Fold into butter mixture, alternating with chocolate and milk.

Spoon mixture on top of nut mixture to two-thirds full. Bake for 30 to 35 minutes, until a skewer inserted in the center of a cupcake tests clean.

Cool in pan for 5 minutes before carefully transferring cupcakes to a wire rack, upside down, to cool completely. Serve cupcakes upside down, with whipped cream.

MUFFIN ESSENTIALS

Muffins are quick to make – ideal for serving to unexpected visitors, and ideal for satisfying a craving for baked treats.

What is the difference between baked (American) and English muffins?

Baked muffins are made by the 'melt and mix' method to produce a cake-like mixture with flavorings. English muffins are round and bread-like, and are made with yeast. They are split open and toasted and are often used as the basis for breakfast recipes, such as eggs benedict.

Perfection

Perfect muffins should have:
- rounded top and straight sides
- tender, 'pebbled', golden crust
- light weight in proportion to size
- slightly coarse but uniform texture

Action

The most important rule of muffin-making is: do not overmix. Overmixed muffins will be tough. Over mixing causes an irregular shape, and a flat, smooth surface.

Stop mixing one stir before you think you need to. Let spooning the mixture into the muffin pan be the final mixing action.

All at once

It is important to place the required amount of mixture into the pan in one go. Hold the mixture on a spoon as close as possible to the pan and push off with a second spoon to give a perfect muffin shape.

Playing with your ingredients

Ingredients for muffins can often be substituted.

- use non-fat milk and yogurt, or buttermilk, instead of regular milk
- use a suitable oil instead of butter
- use honey instead of sugar
- use whole wheat (wholemeal) flour instead of all-purpose (plain) flour

This flexibility allows some creativity, too.

- You can add a little citrus zest, dried fruit, chopped nuts or other ingredients without affecting the success of your muffins.
- Add a little of a fiber component such as old-fashioned rolled oats, and increase wet ingredients slightly to compensate.

Don't defrost frozen berries – use them directly from the freezer so that they don't lose their juiciness when defrosting.

Cool it

When muffins are cooked, it is important to cool them in the pan for about 5 minutes to help prevent them falling apart. Then, turn out onto a wire rack to cool before serving.

Warm it up

To reheat a muffin, first microwave it for 8 seconds on high power, then place in a 325°F (160°C) oven for 5 minutes more, so that the crust is not soggy.

SWEET MUFFINS

COOKING CLASS | BASIC MUFFINS

BASIC MUFFINS

Makes 12

2 cups (250g) all-purpose (plain) flour

2 tsp baking powder

½ cup (110g) superfine (caster) sugar

1 cup fruit (125g) such as diced apple, peach or pear; fresh or frozen berries; currants and golden raisins (sultanas)

⅔ cup (160ml) milk

1 stick (125g) butter, melted

1 egg, lightly beaten

STEP 1
Preheat oven to 350ºF (180ºC). Lightly grease a standard muffin pan or line with paper liners.

STEP 2
Sift flour and baking powder into a large bowl. Stir in sugar and fruit. Make a well in the center of dry ingredients.

STEP 3
Combine milk, butter and egg. Mix into dry ingredients, until just combined.

STEP 4
Spoon into prepared pan to two-thirds full. Bake for 15 to 20 minutes, until a skewer inserted in the center of a muffin tests clean. Cool in pan for 5 minutes, then transfer to a wire rack to cool completely.

BLUEBERRY MUFFINS

Makes 12

2 cups (250g) all-purpose (plain) flour

2 tsp baking powder

½ cup (110g) superfine (caster) sugar

1 cup (125g) fresh or frozen blueberries

⅔ cup (160ml) milk

1 stick (125g) butter, melted

1 egg, lightly beaten

Preheat oven to 350°F (180°C). Grease a standard muffin pan or line with paper liners.

Sift flour, baking powder and sugar into a large bowl. Stir in blueberries. Make a well in center of dry ingredients.

Combine milk, butter and egg. Mix into dry ingredients, until just combined.

Spoon mixture into prepared pan until to two-thirds full. Bake for 15 to 20 minutes, until a skewer inserted in the center of a muffin tests clean.

Cool in pan for 10 minutes, then transfer to a wire rack to cool completely.

COCONUT PLUM MUFFINS

Makes 12

6 Tbsp (90g) butter, softened

1 cup (225g) superfine (caster) sugar

2 eggs

½ tsp coconut extract

½ cup (125ml) yogurt

2½ cups (315g) all-purpose (plain) flour

2½ tsp baking powder

½ cup (125ml) milk

½ cup (45g) unsweetened shredded (desiccated) coconut

1 cup (165g) diced plums, stones removed

¼ cup (25g) unsweetened shredded (desiccated) coconut, for sprinkling

Preheat oven to 350ºF (180ºC). Grease a standard muffin pan or line with paper liners.

Using electric mixer, beat butter and sugar in a bowl until fluffy. Beat in eggs, coconut extract and yogurt.

Sift flour and baking powder over mixture and stir to combine. Add milk and then coconut, stirring just enough to combine. Gently fold in the diced plum.

Spoon mixture into prepared muffin pan. Sprinkle surface of muffins with coconut and bake for 20 to 25 minutes, or until a skewer inserted in the center of a muffin tests clean.

Cool in pan for 5 minutes, then transfer muffins to a wire rack to cool completely.

PEAR BRAN MUFFINS

Makes 12

1 cup (125g) all-purpose (plain) flour

1 tsp baking soda (bicarbonate of soda)

2 tsp baking powder

2 tsp ground ginger

½ tsp salt

2 cups (120g) wheat bran

1 firm ripe pear, peeled and grated

2 eggs

½ cup (125ml) milk

½ cup (125ml) yogurt

½ cup (125ml) vegetable oil

¼ cup (60ml) liquid honey, warmed

¼ cup (55g) sugar

½ tsp vanilla extract

Preheat oven to 400°F (200°C). Grease a standard muffin pan or line with paper liners.

Whisk together flour, baking soda, baking powder, ginger, salt and bran in a large mixing bowl. Add grated pear and toss to combine. Make a well in the center of the dry ingredients.

Whisk eggs with milk, yogurt, oil, honey, sugar and vanilla.

Pour the liquid ingredients into the well in the dry ingredients. Gently mix until just combined.

Spoon mixture into prepared pan. Bake for 15 to 20 minutes, until golden and the top of a muffin springs back when pressed.

Cool in pan for 5 minutes, then transfer muffins to a wire rack to cool completely.

MIXED BERRY & WHITE CHOCOLATE MUFFINS

Makes 12

2½ cups (315g) all-purpose (plain) flour

2½ tsp baking powder

½ cup (110g) firmly packed light brown (soft brown) sugar

½ cup (95g) white chocolate morsels (chips)

2 eggs, lightly beaten

1 cup (250ml) milk

½ cup (125ml) vegetable oil

1½ cups (190g) frozen mixed berries

confectioners' (icing) sugar, for dusting

Preheat oven to 400°F (200°C). Grease a standard muffin pan or line with paper liners.

Whisk together flour, baking powder and brown sugar in a large bowl, then stir in chocolate morsels.

Combine eggs, milk and oil, and stir into the flour mixture, until just combined. Fold in berries.

Spoon mixture evenly into prepared pan.

Bake for 20 minutes, until a skewer inserted in the center of a muffin tests clean. Stand muffins in pan for 5 minutes, then transfer to a wire rack to cool completely.

Dust muffins with confectioners' sugar before serving.

LEMON POPPYSEED MUFFINS

Makes 12

1 stick (125g) butter, softened

1/2 cup (110g) superfine (caster) sugar

2 eggs

1 cup (250ml) yogurt

finely grated zest of 1 lemon

1/2 cup (125ml) fresh lemon juice

1/3 cup (50g) poppyseeds

2 cups (250g) all-purpose (plain) flour

2 tsp baking powder

1/4 tsp baking soda (bicarbonate of soda)

Lemon syrup
juice and zest of 4 lemons

3/4 cup (170g) superfine (caster) sugar

Preheat oven to 400°F (200°C). Grease a standard muffin pan or line with paper liners.

Using an electric mixer, beat butter and sugar together until fluffy. Beat in eggs, one at a time, then beat in yogurt, lemon zest and juice and poppyseeds.

Sift the flour, baking powder and baking soda over butter mixture. Fold together just to combine into a smooth batter, taking care not to overmix.

Spoon the mixture into the prepared muffin pan. Bake for 20 minutes, or until muffins are pale golden and a skewer inserted in the center of a muffin tests clean. Cool in pan for 5 minutes.

To make lemon syrup, combine lemon zest and juice and sugar in a saucepan, stirring until sugar dissolves. Bring to a boil and boil steadily for 2 minutes.

Carefully remove muffins from pan and transfer to a shallow tray, then spoon hot lemon syrup over them. Leave muffins for 20 minutes to allow syrup to soak in. Serve muffins with any extra syrup spooned over them.

DOUBLE CHOCOLATE MUFFINS

Makes 12

2 cups (250g) all-purpose (plain) flour

2 tsp baking powder

¼ cup (30g) unsweetened cocoa powder

1 cup (190g) chopped semisweet (plain) chocolate

3 Tbsp superfine (caster) sugar

¾ cup (190ml) milk

½ cup (115g) sour cream

6 Tbsp (90g) butter, melted

1 egg, lightly beaten

Chocolate frosting
1½ cups (225g) confectioners' (icing) sugar, sifted

3 Tbsp unsweetened cocoa powder

1 Tbsp (15g) butter, melted

about 3 Tbsp boiling water

Preheat oven to 350°F (180°C). Lightly grease a standard muffin pan lightly or line with paper liners.

Sift flour, baking powder and cocoa powder into a large bowl. Stir in chocolate and sugar. Make a well in center of dry ingredients.

Combine milk, sour cream, butter and egg. Mix into dry ingredients, until just combined.

Spoon into prepared pan to two-thirds full. Bake for 15 to 20 minutes, until the center of a muffin springs back when pressed. Cool in pan for a few minutes, then transfer muffins to a wire rack to cool completely.

To make chocolate frosting, beat together all ingredients in a bowl, adding just enough water to make a smooth and spreadable consistency. Frost cooled muffins.

SPICED DATE MUFFINS

Makes 12

1 ¾ cups (220g) all-purpose (plain) flour

1 ¾ tsp baking powder

1 tsp baking soda (bicarbonate of soda)

1 tsp ground ginger

1 tsp ground cinnamon

6 ½ Tbsp (100g) butter, chopped

⅓ cup (75g) firmly packed light brown (soft brown) sugar

1 cup (160g) chopped pitted dates

1 egg, lightly beaten

1 cup (250ml) buttermilk (or unsweetened natural yogurt)

⅓ cup (55g) crystallized ginger, finely chopped

Preheat oven to 375°F (190°C). Grease a standard muffin pan or line with paper liners.

Sift flour, baking powder, baking soda, ginger and cinnamon into a bowl and make a well in the center.

Place butter, sugar and dates in a saucepan over a low heat. Stir continuously until the butter melts. Pour the date mixture into the dry ingredients, and add the egg, buttermilk and crystallized ginger. Stir until just combined.

Spoon mixture into prepared pan. Bake for 25 minutes, until a skewer inserted in the center of a muffin tests clean.

Cool in pan for 5 minutes, then transfer muffins to a wire rack to cool completely.

APRICOT BRAN MUFFINS

Makes 9

1 cup (60g) wheat bran

1 cup (250ml) milk, hot

1 apple, peeled, cored and grated

½ cup (80g) roughly chopped dried apricots

1 egg, lightly beaten

⅓ cup (75g) light brown (soft brown) sugar

4 tsp vegetable oil

1 cup (125g) all-purpose (plain) flour

2 tsp baking powder

Place bran in a large bowl. Pour over hot milk. Set aside for 1 hour.

Preheat oven to 400ºF (200ºC). Line a standard muffin pan with nine paper liners.

Add apple, apricot, egg, sugar and oil to bran mixture. Stir to combine. Sift flour and baking powder into mixture and stir gently, until just combined.

Spoon into prepared liners. Bake for 20 to 25 minutes, until a skewer inserted in the center of a muffin tests clean. Transfer to a wire rack to cool.

PEACHES & CREAM MUFFINS

Makes 12

½ stick (65g) butter, softened

½ cup (110g) superfine (caster) sugar

2 eggs

1 tsp vanilla extract

½ cup (115g) sour cream

1 cup (125ml) peach yogurt

finely grated zest of 1 lemon

14oz (400g) can peach slices, drained and roughly chopped

2½ cups (315g) all-purpose (plain) flour

2½ tsp baking powder

2oz (60g) cream cheese

¼ cup (55g) superfine (caster) sugar, for sprinkling

Preheat oven to 350°F (180°C). Grease a standard muffin pan or line with paper liners.

Using an electric mixer, beat butter and sugar until fluffy. Beat in eggs, vanilla, sour cream and yogurt.

Stir in lemon zest and chopped peaches. Then sift flour and baking powder onto mixture and gently stir to just combine.

Divide mixture among prepared muffin pans, placing a teaspoonful of cream cheese in the center of each muffin. Sprinkle tops of muffins with sugar.

Bake for 25 minutes, until firm to the touch and golden brown. Cool muffins in pan for 5 minutes, then transfer to a wire rack to cool completely.

BUTTERMILK RAISIN MUFFINS

Makes 12

1 cup (125g) all-purpose (plain) flour

1 cup (125g) whole wheat (wholemeal) flour

⅓ cup (75g) superfine (caster) sugar

4 tsp baking powder

1½ tsp ground cinnamon

½ cup (80g) golden raisins (sultanas)

1 egg

1½ cups (375ml) buttermilk

¼ cup (60ml) vegetable oil

1 Tbsp superfine (caster) sugar, for dusting

1 tsp ground cinnamon, for dusting

Preheat oven to 400°F (200°C). Lightly grease a standard muffin pan or line with paper liners.

Whisk together flours, sugar, baking powder and cinnamon in a bowl. Add golden raisins. Whisk together egg, buttermilk and oil and fold into dry ingredients, until just combined.

Spoon mixture into prepared pan. Dust well with combined sugar and ground cinnamon.

Bake for 15 to 20 minutes, until golden and a skewer inserted in the center of a muffin tests clean.

Cool in pan for 5 minutes, then transfer muffins to a wire rack to cool completely.

HONEY & OAT MUFFINS

Makes 12

1 ½ cups (190g) all-purpose (plain) flour

1 cup (125g) whole wheat (wholemeal) flour

2 ½ tsp baking powder

1 cup (225g) superfine (caster) sugar

1 cup (90g) old-fashioned rolled oats

6 Tbsp (90g) butter

¼ cup (60ml) liquid honey

1 ¼ cups (310ml) buttermilk

1 egg, lightly beaten

Preheat oven to 350°F (180°C). Lightly grease a standard muffin pan or line with paper liners.

Sift flours and baking powder into a large bowl. Stir in sugar and three-fourths of the oats.

Melt butter and honey together in a small saucepan over low heat. Cool slightly.

Combine buttermilk and egg.

Make a well in the center of the dry ingredients. Pour in butter and honey mixture. Add buttermilk mixture all at once. Mix lightly, until just combined.

Spoon mixture evenly into prepared pan. Sprinkle top of muffins with remaining oats.

Bake 20 to 25 minutes, until a skewer inserted in the center of a muffin tests clean. Cool in pan 5 minutes. Transfer muffins to a wire rack to cool further. Serve muffins while still warm, or reheat gently just before serving.

DOUBLE GINGER PEAR MUFFINS

Makes 12

2 cups (250g) all-purpose (plain) flour

2 tsp baking powder

¾ cup (170g) superfine (caster) sugar

1 tsp ground ginger

pinch of salt

2 peeled ripe pears, cored and diced

⅓ cup (55g) crystallized ginger, finely chopped

2 eggs

½ cup (125ml) milk + a little extra, if needed

2 Tbsp (30g) melted butter

juice and finely grated zest of 1 orange

⅓ cup (55g) crystallized ginger, thinly sliced

Preheat oven to 375°F (190°C). Grease a standard muffin pan or line with paper liners.

Sift flour, baking powder, sugar, ground ginger and salt into a bowl. Add diced pears and crystallized ginger and toss together. Make a well in the center.

In another bowl, whisk together eggs, milk, butter, orange juice and zest. Pour wet ingredients into dry ingredients and stir just enough to combine, adding a little more milk, if necessary, to create a smooth batter.

Spoon mixture into prepared muffin pan and sprinkle tops of muffins with extra sliced ginger. Bake for 15 to 20 minutes, until a skewer inserted in the center of a muffin tests clean.

Cool in pan for 5 minutes, then transfer muffins to a wire rack to cool completely.

APPLE & PECAN MUFFINS

Makes 12

2 cups (250g) all-purpose (plain) flour

2 tsp baking powder

1 tsp ground cinnamon

½ cup (110g) light brown (soft brown) sugar

2 small green-skinned apples, peeled, cored, finely chopped

⅓ cup (45g) pecans, chopped, + extra ¼ cup (35g), chopped

⅔ cup (160ml) milk

1 stick (125g) butter, melted

1 egg, lightly beaten

Preheat oven to 350°F (180°C). Line a standard muffin pan with paper liners.

Sift flour, baking powder and cinnamon into a large bowl. Stir in sugar, apple and pecans.

Whisk together milk, butter and egg. Make a well in the center of the dry ingredients. Add milk mixture all at once. Mix lightly until just combined, taking care not to overmix.

Spoon mixture evenly into prepared liners. Sprinkle tops of muffins with extra chopped pecans.

Bake for 20 to 25 minutes, until a skewer inserted in the center of a muffin tests clean.

Cool in pan for 5 minutes, then transfer to a wire rack to cool a little more. Serve muffins while still warm, or reheat gently just before serving.

BIRCHER MUESLI MUFFINS

Makes 12

1¾ cups (220g) all-purpose (plain) flour

1¾ tsp baking powder

½ cup (110g) light brown (soft brown) sugar

½ tsp pumpkin pie spice (mixed spice)

1½ cups (135g) untoasted muesli, + extra, for sprinkling

½ cup (125ml) plain yogurt

¼ cup (60ml) milk

¼ cup (60ml) canola oil

1 egg

1 green-skinned apple, skin on, cored, grated

Preheat oven to 350°F (180°C). Line a standard muffin pan with paper liners or spray with oil.

In a large mixing bowl, whisk together flour, baking powder, sugar and spice. Stir in muesli. Make a well in the center of dry ingredients.

Whisk together yogurt, milk, oil and egg. Add to the dry ingredients with apple, mixing lightly, until just combined.

Spoon mixture into cases to two-thirds full. Sprinkle tops of muffins with extra muesli. Bake for 20 to 25 minutes, until a skewer inserted in the center of a muffin tests clean.

Cool muffins in pan for 5 minutes, then transfer to a wire rack to cool completely.

STICKY DATE MUFFINS

Makes 12

1 cup (160g) chopped, pitted dates

¾ cup (180ml) fresh orange juice

2 eggs, lightly beaten

4 Tbsp light corn syrup

2 Tbsp molasses

¼ cup (60ml) vegetable oil

2¼ cups (285g) all-purpose (plain) flour

2¼ tsp baking powder

⅓ cup (45g) chopped shelled natural pistachios

¼ cup (50g) semisweet (plain) chocolate morsels (chips)

confectioners' (icing) sugar, for dusting

Preheat oven to 350°F (180°C). Line a standard muffin pan with paper liners.

Place dates and orange juice in a microwave-safe bowl. Microwave, covered, on high (100%) power for 1 minute. Set aside for 10 minutes.

Transfer date mixture to a large bowl. Mix in eggs, corn syrup, molasses and oil, until combined.

Sift flour and baking powder into a small bowl. Fold flour mixture, pistachios and chocolate into date mixture.

Spoon the mixture evenly into prepared liners. Bake for 20 to 25 minutes, until a skewer inserted in the center of a muffin tests clean.

Allow to cool in the pan for 5 minutes, then transfer to a wire rack to cool completely. Dust with confectioners' sugar before serving.

BANANA MUFFINS WITH PISTACHIO CRUMBLE

Makes 18

2 cups (250g) all-purpose (plain) flour

2 tsp baking powder

¼ tsp baking soda (bicarbonate of soda)

¾ cup (170g) firmly packed light brown (soft brown) sugar

1 stick (125g) butter, melted

¾ cup (170g) mashed ripe banana

¾ cup (175g) sour cream

2 eggs, lightly beaten

4 tsp milk

Pistachio crumble

¾ cup (95g) chopped shelled natural pistachios

3 Tbsp light brown (soft brown) sugar

Preheat oven to 350ºF (180ºC). Lightly grease 18 holes of two standard muffin pans.

Sift flour, baking powder and baking soda into a large bowl. Whisk in sugar.

Combine butter, banana, sour cream, eggs and milk. Fold gently into flour mixture. Do not overmix.

To make the pistachio crumble, combine pistachios and sugar in a bowl.

Spoon muffin mixture into prepared pans to two-thirds full. Sprinkle each muffin with pistachio crumble.

Bake for 15 to 20 minutes, until a skewer inserted in the center of a muffin tests clean.

Cool muffins in pans for 5 minutes, then transfer to a wire rack to cool completely.

APPLE & OAT MUFFINS

Makes 12

1½ cups (190g) all-purpose (plain) flour

1½ tsp baking powder

¾ cup (90g) firmly packed light brown (soft brown) sugar

1½ tsp ground cinnamon

1 cup (170g) old-fashioned rolled oats

2 medium green-skinned apples, unpeeled, grated

1 egg, lightly beaten

1 cup (250ml) soy milk

⅓ cup (80ml) canola oil

Oat streusel

⅓ cup (45g) all-purpose (plain) flour

½ tsp ground cinnamon

2½ Tbsp (40g) cold butter, chopped

3 Tbsp light brown (soft brown) sugar

3 Tbsp old-fashioned rolled oats

1 tsp water

Preheat oven to 400°F (200°C). Grease a standard muffin pan.

To make oat streusel, whisk together flour and cinnamon in a small bowl. Rub in butter using fingertips, until the mixture resembles breadcrumbs. Stir in sugar, rolled oats and water, until combined.

To make muffin batter, whisk together flour, baking powder, sugar and cinnamon in a bowl. Add oats and apple and mix well. Add egg, soy milk and oil. Stir until just combined. Spoon mixture into prepared pan, then sprinkle with oat streusel.

Bake for about 20 minutes, until a skewer inserted in the center of a muffin tests clean. Stand in pan for 5 minutes, then transfer to a wire rack to cool.

COCONUT RASPBERRY MUFFINS

Makes 12

2 cups (250g) all-purpose (plain) flour

2 tsp baking powder

1 cup (225g) superfine (caster) sugar

½ cup (45g) unsweetened shredded (desiccated) coconut

2 tsp finely grated lime zest + extra, for decorating

1 cup (125g) fresh or frozen raspberries + extra, for decorating

1 cup (250ml) canned coconut milk

½ cup (125ml) vegetable oil

1 egg, lightly beaten

⅓ cup (30g) unsweetened coconut flakes

Preheat oven to 375°F (190°C). Line a standard muffin pan with paper liners.

Sift flour, baking powder and sugar into a large bowl. Stir in shredded coconut and lime zest. Make a well in the center; add raspberries.

Combine coconut milk, oil and egg. Pour coconut milk mixture into well in dry ingredients and mix gently, until almost combined, taking care not to overmix.

Spoon mixture evenly into prepared liners. Sprinkle tops of muffins with coconut flakes, gently pressing coconut into batter.

Bake muffins for about 25 minutes, until a skewer inserted in the center of a muffin tests clean. Cool muffins in pan for 5 minutes, then transfer to a wire rack to cool further.

Serve muffins warm or at room temperature. Decorate with extra lime zest and raspberries.

CREAM CHEESE & APRICOT STREUSEL MUFFINS

Makes 12

½ cup (125ml) light olive oil

½ cup (110g) superfine (caster) sugar

2 eggs

1 cup (250ml) buttermilk

finely grated zest of 1 orange

1 cup (160g) chopped dried apricots

2½ cups (315g) all-purpose (plain) flour

2½ tsp baking powder

¼ tsp baking soda (bicarbonate of soda)

2oz (60g) cream cheese

Streusel topping
2 Tbsp light brown (soft brown) sugar

2 Tbsp chopped walnuts

2 Tbsp (30g) butter, melted

1 tsp ground cinnamon

Preheat oven to 400°C (200°C). Grease standard muffin pan or line with paper liners.

In a large mixing bowl, combine the oil, sugar, eggs, buttermilk and orange zest, stirring well. Gently stir in dried apricots.

Sift flour, baking powder and baking soda over wet mixture and fold in just enough to combine.

Spoon mixture into prepared muffin pan, placing a tcaspoon of cream cheese in the center of each muffin.

To make streusel topping, combine ingredients in a bowl and sprinkle a little over each muffin.

Bake for 20 to 25 minutes, until pale golden and the center of a muffin springs back when pressed.

Cool in pan for 5 minutes, then transfer to a wire rack to cool completely.

BANANA & OATBRAN MUFFINS

Makes 12

6 Tbsp (90g) butter, softened

⅓ cup firmly packed light brown (soft brown) sugar

1 egg

¾ cup (95g) all-purpose (plain) flour

1 ¾ tsp baking powder

½ cup (115g) mashed ripe banana

¾ cup (70g) oatbran

½ cup (125ml) buttermilk

¾ cup (95g) chopped pecans

Preheat oven to 350°F (180°C). Line a standard muffin pan with paper liners, or spray with oil.

Using electric mixer, beat butter and sugar together until fluffy. Beat in egg until combined.

Sift flour and baking powder together. Fold in the butter mixture with banana, oatbran and buttermilk, stirring only until combined.

Spoon mixture into cases to two-thirds full. Sprinkle tops of muffins with pecans.

Bake for 20 to 25 minutes, until a skewer inserted in the center of a muffin tests clean.

Cool muffins in pan for 5 minutes, then transfer to a wire rack to cool completely.

Muffin note Ripe bananas can be frozen until ready to use, then defrosted. Don't worry about the skin going black; the banana flesh is still perfectly good for cooking.

APPLE & RASPBERRY MUFFINS

Makes 12

2 cups (250g) all-purpose (plain) flour

2 tsp baking soda (bicarbonate of soda)

1 cup (225g) superfine (caster) sugar

1 cup (250ml) pouring cream (or milk)

¼ cup (60ml) vegetable oil

3 tsp vanilla extract

1 apple, cored, peeled, thinly sliced

4oz (100g) fresh raspberries

1 Tbsp flaked almonds

confectioners' (icing) sugar, for dusting

Preheat oven to 350ºF (180ºC). Line a standard muffin pan with paper liners.

Sift flour and baking soda together into a bowl.

In another bowl, combine sugar, cream, oil and vanilla. Fold in sifted flour and baking soda.

Spoon mixture into prepared liners to two-thirds full. Top with sliced apple, raspberries and almonds.

Bake for 25 to 30 minutes, until a skewer inserted in the center of a muffin tests clean.

Cool in pan for 5 minutes, then transfer to a wire rack to cool completely.

Dust with confectioners' sugar before serving.

APRICOT, ALMOND & HONEY MUFFINS

Makes 12

1 cup (125g) all-purpose (plain) flour

1 ½ teaspoon baking powder

1 cup (90g) old-fashioned rolled oats + extra, for sprinkling

½ cup (60g) almond meal

½ cup (80g) finely chopped dried apricots

¾ cup (180ml) low-fat milk

¼ cup (65ml) mild liquid honey

4 Tbsp (60g) low-fat spread or butter, melted

1 egg

confectioners' (icing) sugar, for dusting

Preheat oven to 350°F (180°C). Line a standard muffin pan with paper liners.

Sift flour and baking powder into a large bowl. Mix in oats, almond meal and apricots. Make a well in the center of the dry ingredients.

Whisk together milk, honey, low-fat spread and egg. Add to dry ingredients, mixing lightly, until just combined.

Spoon mixture into cases to two-thirds full. Sprinkle tops of muffins with extra oats. Bake for 20 to 25 minutes, until a skewer inserted in the center of a muffin tests clean.

Cool muffins in pan for 5 minutes, then transfer to a wire rack to cool completely.

Serve dusted with confectioners' sugar.

APPLESAUCE MUESLI MUFFINS

Makes 10

1 egg, lightly beaten

1 Tbsp vegetable oil

½ cup (125ml) canned unsweetened applesauce

1 cup (250ml) apple juice

1 cup (160g) chopped, pitted dates

¾ cup (70g) untoasted muesli

1 cup (125g) all-purpose (plain) flour

1 tsp ground cinnamon

1 tsp baking powder

1 tsp baking soda (bicarbonate of soda)

Topping
2 Tbsp raw (turbinado) sugar

½ tsp ground cinnamon

Preheat oven to 375°F (190°C). Lightly grease 10 holes of a standard muffin pan or line with paper liners.

Place egg, oil, applesauce, apple juice, dates and muesli in a bowl and stir well to combine.

Sift flour, cinnamon, baking powder and baking soda into another bowl and make a well in the center. Pour apple mixture into the well and stir briefly, just to combine.

Spoon mixture into prepared muffin pan.

To make topping, combine raw sugar with cinnamon and sprinkle a little over each muffin. Bake for 15 to 20 minutes, until center of a muffin springs back when lightly pressed.

Cool in pan for 5 minutes, then transfer to a wire rack to cool completely.

BANANA CHOC CHIP MUFFINS

Makes 12

3 ripe bananas, mashed

½ cup (110g) sugar

7 Tbsp (100g) butter, melted

1 egg, beaten

2 Tbsp milk

1½ cups (190g) all-purpose (plain) flour

1 tsp baking soda (bicarbonate of soda)

1 tsp baking powder

1½ cups (250g) semisweet (plain) chocolate morsels (chips)

Preheat oven to 375ºF (190ºC). Grease a standard muffin pan or line with paper liners.

In a bowl, place mashed bananas, sugar, melted butter, egg and milk and stir to combine.

Sift flour, baking powder and baking soda onto banana mixture and stir to just combine. Fold in chocolate.

Spoon the mixture into prepared pan and bake for 20 to 25 minutes, until golden brown and the center of a muffin springs back when pressed.

Cool in pan for 5 minutes, then transfer to a wire rack to cool completely.

CHOCOLATE BLUEBERRY MUFFINS

Makes 12

1 ¾ cups (220g)
all-purpose (plain) flour

4 tsp baking powder

¼ cup (30g) unsweetened
cocoa powder

½ cup (110g) superfine
(caster) sugar

½ cup (95g) semisweet
(plain) chocolate morsels
(chips)

1 cup (250ml) milk

1 egg, lightly beaten

¼ cup (60ml) canola oil

1 cup (125g) frozen or fresh
blueberries

Preheat oven to 400ºF (200ºC). Grease a standard muffin pan or line with paper liners.

Sift the flour, baking powder and cocoa powder into a bowl and stir in the sugar and chocolate. Make a well in the center.

Combine milk, egg and oil and pour into the well, then add with the blueberries. Mix to just combine, taking care not to overmix.

Spoon mixture into prepared pan and bake for 25 minutes, until golden brown and springy to the touch.

Cool in pan for 5 minutes, then transfer to a wire rack to cool completely.

MOCHACCINO MUFFINS

Makes 12

1 ¼ sticks (150g) butter, softened

1 cup (225g) superfine (caster) sugar

2 eggs

1 ½ cups (375ml) plain yogurt

1 Tbsp instant coffee granules mixed with 1 Tbsp boiling water

2 ½ cups (315g) all-purpose (plain) flour

2 ½ tsp baking powder

¾ cup (145g) semisweet (plain) chocolate morsels (chips)

Cocoa swirl

4 Tbsp (60g) butter, melted

2 Tbsp unsweetened cocoa powder, sifted

2 Tbsp light brown (soft brown) sugar

Preheat oven to 400ºF (200ºC). Grease two Texas muffin pans.

First, to make the cocoa swirl, combine melted butter with cocoa powder and brown sugar. Set aside.

To make the muffins, use an electric mixer to beat butter and sugar until fluffy. Beat in the eggs, one at a time, then beat in the yogurt and coffee mixture.

Sift the flour and baking powder over the mixture, gently stirring just enough to combine into a smooth mixture. Fold in chocolate.

Spoon mixture into prepared pans. Spoon cocoa swirl on top and swirl this into each muffin with a skewer.

Bake for 25 to 30 minutes, until a skewer inserted in the center of a muffin tests clean.

Cool in pans for 5 minutes, then transfer to a wire rack to cool further. Serve muffins warm or at room temperature.

MIXED BERRY OAT MUFFINS

Makes 9

1 ½ cups (190g)
all-purpose (plain) flour

1 ½ tsp baking powder

½ cup (45g) oatbran

¾ cup (170g) firmly packed
light brown (soft brown)
sugar

1 cup (250ml) buttermilk

2 Tbsp vegetable oil

1 egg, lightly beaten

1 ½ cups (190g) fresh or
frozen mixed berries

confectioners' (icing) sugar,
for dusting

Preheat oven to 350°F (180°C). Cut nine squares of parchment paper 5 x 5 inches (13 cm x 13 cm). Lightly grease nine holes of a standard muffin pan. Line with paper squares.

In a large bowl, combine sifted flour and baking powder with oat bran and sugar.

Combine buttermilk, oil and egg. Stir gently into flour mixture. Fold berries through, until combined, taking care not to overmix.

Spoon mixture into prepared pan. Bake for 20 to 25 minutes, or until a skewer inserted in the center of a muffin tests clean.

Cool muffins in pan for 5 minutes, then transfer to a wire rack to cool completely.

Serve dusted with confectioners' sugar.

TROPICAL FRUIT MUFFINS

Makes 12

¼ cup (60ml) canola oil

½ cup (110g) raw (turbinado) sugar

2 eggs

1 tsp vanilla extract

1 cup (180g) drained canned crushed pineapple

2 mashed bananas

½ cup (80g) chopped dried papaya or mango

3 cups (375g) all-purpose (plain) flour

3 tsp baking powder

Preheat oven to 350ºF (180ºC). Lightly grease a standard muffin pan or line with paper liners.

In a large bowl, beat together the oil, sugar, eggs and vanilla. Stir in pineapple, mashed banana and dried papaya or mango.

Sift the flour and baking powder into the bowl and stir, just enough to combine into a smooth batter.

Spoon into prepared pan and bake for 20 minutes, until puffed and golden brown.

Cool in pan for 5 minutes, then transfer to a wire rack to cool completely.

WHOLE WHEAT KIWI MUFFINS

Makes 12

5 kiwifruit, peeled

1 cup (125g) all-purpose (plain) flour

2 ½ tsp baking powder

¾ cup (90g) whole wheat (wholemeal) flour

¼ cup (55g) superfine (caster) sugar

¾ cup (180ml) milk

5 Tbsp (75g) butter, melted

1 egg, lightly beaten

apricot jelly (jam), for glazing

Preheat oven to 400°F (200°C). Line a standard muffin pan with paper liners.

Cut three kiwifruit into four slices each. Roughly chop remaining two.

Whisk together dry ingredients in a large bowl. Make a well in the center.

Combine milk, butter, egg and chopped kiwifruit. Pour into well in dry ingredients. Stir gently with a fork until mixture is just combined.

Spoon into paper liners and top each muffin with a slice of kiwifruit. Bake for 20 minutes, brush with a little warmed apricot jam and bake for another 5 minutes, until center of muffins spring back when pressed.

Cool in pan for 5 minutes, then transfer to a wire rack to cool completely.

SUGARED RHUBARB MUFFINS

Makes 12

1 egg

2 Tbsp vegetable oil

⅓ cup (75g) superfine (caster) sugar

1 cup (250ml) milk

¼ cup (60g) sour cream

1 tsp vanilla extract

2 cups (250g) all-purpose (plain) flour

2¼ tsp baking soda (bicarbonate of soda)

½ tsp ground cinnamon

1½ cups (180g) diced fresh rhubarb

¼ cup (55g) raw (turbinado) sugar, for sprinkling

Preheat oven to 400°F (200°C). Line a standard muffin pan with paper liners.

Place egg in a bowl and beat lightly. Add oil, sugar, milk, sour cream and vanilla and stir to combine.

Sift the flour, baking soda and cinnamon into a large bowl. Make a well in the center and pour the wet ingredients and the rhubarb into the well. Stir just enough to combine.

Spoon batter into prepared liners to three-fourths full. Sprinkle with raw sugar.

Bake for 25 minutes, until golden brown and a skewer inserted in the center of a muffin tests clean.

Cool in pan for 5 minutes, then transfer to a wire rack to cool completely.

CHERRY CHEESECAKE MUFFINS

Makes 12

1 stick (125g) butter, softened

½ cup (110g) superfine (caster) sugar

2 eggs

1 cup (250ml) milk

¼ cup (60ml) lemon juice

2½ cups (315g) all-purpose (plain) flour

2½ tsp baking powder

4oz (125g) cream cheese

1 cup (150g) pitted cherries

confectioners' (icing) sugar, for dusting

Preheat oven to 400°F (200°C). Grease a standard muffin pan or line with paper liners.

Using electric mixer, beat butter and sugar until fluffy. Beat in the eggs, then stir in the milk and lemon juice.

Sift the flour and baking powder over the butter mixture then fold in to form a batter.

Spoon half of the muffin batter into the base of prepared pan, then add 1 teaspoon of cream cheese and three cherries per muffin. Top with the remaining muffin batter.

Bake for 20 to 25 minutes, until golden brown and the center of a muffin springs back when pressed.

Cool in pan for 5 minutes, then transfer to a wire rack to cool completely.

Dust with confectioners' sugar before serving.

LEMON SYRUP PISTACHIO MUFFINS

Makes 12

6 Tbsp (100g) butter, softened

½ cup (110g) superfine (caster) sugar

1 egg

1 Tbsp finely grated lemon zest

½ cup (65g) chopped shelled natural pistachios

½ cup (45g) unsweetened shredded (desiccated) coconut

2 cups (250g) all-purpose (plain) flour

2 tsp baking powder

1 cup (250ml) buttermilk

whipped cream, for serving

mint leaves, for serving

Lemon syrup

1 cup (225g) superfine (caster) sugar

⅔ cup (170ml) water

½ cup (125ml) fresh lemon juice

shredded zest of 3 lemons

Preheat oven to 375ºF (190ºC). Grease a standard muffin pan or line with paper liners.

Using an electric mixer, beat butter and sugar until fluffy. Add egg and zest and beat until combined.

Stir in pistachios and coconut. Sift flour and baking powder into a small bowl. Fold half of the flour mixture into the butter mixture, then alternate remaining flour mixture with buttermilk until just combined, taking care not to overmix.

Spoon mixture into prepared pan. Bake for about 20 minutes, until a skewer inserted in the center of a muffin tests clean. Leave muffins in pan and prepare lemon syrup.

To make lemon syrup, combine ingredients in a medium-sized saucepan. Stir over a low heat until sugar dissolves. Bring to a boil, and simmer, without stirring, for about 4 minutes, until syrup thickens slightly.

Pour one-fourth of the syrup over warm muffins in pan. Leave for 10 minutes, then carefully remove muffins from pan.

When ready to serve, pour remaining syrup over muffins. Serve with whipped cream and decorate with mint leaves.

ALMOND & CARAMEL PEAR MUFFINS

Makes 12

1 ¼ cups (160g) all-purpose (plain) flour

1 ¼ tsp baking powder

½ cup (110g) superfine (caster) sugar

2 tsp ground cinnamon

¾ cup (90g) almond meal

⅓ cup (45g) blanched almonds, chopped and toasted

½ cup (125ml) milk

1 stick (125g) butter, melted

2 eggs

1 tsp vanilla extract

Caramel pear

2 Tbsp (30g) butter

⅓ cup (75g) light brown (soft brown) sugar

1 firm ripe pear, peeled, cored, thinly sliced

Preheat oven to 350ºF (180ºC). Lightly grease a standard muffin pan.

First, to make caramel pear, combine butter and sugar in a skillet (fry-pan) on medium heat. Add pear and cook, turning, for about 5 minutes, until just tender. Remove pear slices from caramel, reserving both, and cool to room temperature.

To make cake batter, sift flour, baking powder, sugar and cinnamon into a bowl. Stir in almond meal and almonds.

Whisk together milk, butter, eggs and vanilla.

Make a well in the center of dry ingredients. Add milk mixture all at once. Fold half of the cooked pear slices into the batter. Mix lightly until just combined, taking care not to overmix. Spoon muffin mixture into prepared pan. Top muffins with remaining pear slices.

Bake for 20 to 25 minutes, until a skewer inserted in the center of a muffin tests clean. Cool in pan for 5 minutes, then transfer to a wire rack to cool completely. Spoon remaining caramel over muffins, to serve.

BAKED MUFFIN PUDDING

Serves 6

6 prepared Banana Choc Chip Muffins (see page 148) or other sweet muffins

1¼ cups (310ml) pouring cream

1¼ cups (310ml) milk

4 eggs

⅓ cup (75g) superfine (caster) sugar

1 tsp vanilla extract

¼ tsp ground nutmeg

¼ tsp ground cinnamon

ice cream (optional), for serving

Preheat oven to 350°F (180°C). Lightly grease a 6-cup capacity (1.5L) ovenproof dish.

Slice muffins into ¼ inch (6mm) slices. Arrange in prepared ovenproof dish.

Whisk together cream, milk, eggs, sugar and vanilla. Pour over muffins. Sprinkle with ground nutmeg and cinnamon.

Place dish in a roasting pan, and add enough warm water to roasting pan to come halfway up side of dish. Bake for about 55 minutes, until firm. Immediately remove the dish from the pan of water. Serve pudding hot, with ice cream if desired.

SAVORY
MUFFINS

CHEDDAR, ZUCCHINI & CORN MUFFINS

Makes 12

1 ¾ cups (220g)
all-purpose (plain) flour

2 ¾ tsp baking powder

1 zucchini (courgette),
trimmed and grated

5oz (140g) canned corn
(kernels), drained

½ cup (60g) grated
cheddar

4 tsp chopped parsley

¾ cup (190ml) milk

6 Tbsp (90g) butter, melted

1 egg

Preheat oven to 350°F (180°C). Lightly grease a standard muffin pan or line with paper liners.

Sift the flour and baking powder together into a bowl. Add zucchini, corn, cheese and parsley, and mix until well combined.

Whisk together milk, butter and egg. Add mixture to dry ingredients and stir gently, until just combined (mixture should still be lumpy).

Spoon mixture into muffin pan to two-thirds full. Bake for 20 to 25 minutes, until golden and springy to the touch.

Cool in pan for 5 minutes, then transfer to a wire rack to cool further. Serve warm, or reheat gently before serving.

ZUCCHINI CORNBREAD MUFFINS

Makes 12

1 cup (150g) all-purpose (plain) flour

1 cup (170g) medium yellow cornmeal (polenta)

4 tsp sugar

4 tsp baking powder

1 egg

½ cup (125ml) milk

¼ cup (60ml) vegetable oil

10oz (285g) canned creamed corn

2 small zucchini (courgettes), grated

Preheat oven to 400°F (200°C). Lightly grease a standard muffin pan or line with paper liners.

Sift the flour, cornmeal, sugar and baking powder into a large bowl.

Combine egg, milk, oil and corn in another bowl. Add the zucchini and wet ingredients to flour mixture and stir until just combined.

Spoon into prepared pan. Bake for 15 to 20 minutes, until golden and a skewer inserted in the center of a muffin tests clean.

Cool in pan for 5 minutes, then transfer to a wire rack. Serve warm, or reheat gently just before serving.

BELL PEPPER & GRUYÈRE MUFFINS

Makes 18

2 cups (250g) all-purpose (plain) flour

1 ½ teaspoons baking powder

½ tsp baking soda (bicarbonate of soda)

¼ tsp chili powder

½ tsp salt

¼ cup (40g) medium cornmeal (polenta)

2 cups (240g) grated gruyère

3 scallions (spring onions), finely chopped

1 red bell pepper (capsicum), deseeded and diced

1 ¼ cups (310ml) buttermilk

4 Tbsp (60g) butter, melted

2 large eggs, lightly beaten

Preheat oven to 425ºF (220ºC). Lightly grease 18 holes of two standard muffin pans or line with paper liners.

Sift flour, baking powder, baking soda, chili powder and salt into a bowl. Stir in cornmeal, gruyère, scallion and pepper.

Combine buttermilk, butter and egg. Gently fold buttermilk mixture into flour mixture, until just combined, taking care not to overmix.

Spoon into prepared pans and bake for 20 minutes, until golden and springy to the touch.

Cool in pan for 5 minutes, then transfer to a wire rack. Serve warm, or reheat gently before serving.

PUMPKIN, FETA & PINENUT MUFFINS

Makes 12

6 slices prosciutto, halved crosswise

11oz (300g) pumpkin, cut into small dice

olive oil, for cooking

2 cups (250g) all-purpose (plain) flour

2 tsp baking powder

5oz (150g) feta, crumbled

¼ cup (10 g) chopped basil

¾ cup (190ml) milk

½ cup (125ml) vegetable oil

1 egg, lightly beaten

¼ cup (35g) pinenuts

Preheat oven to 350°F (180°C). Lightly grease a standard muffin pan. Line pan with prosciutto.

Toss pumpkin with a little olive oil in a roasting pan. Roast for 20 to 25 minutes, until tender. Set aside to cool.

Sift flour and baking powder into a large mixing bowl. Add pumpkin, feta and basil. Mix well.

Whisk together milk, oil and egg. Season to taste.

Make a well in the center of dry ingredients. Add milk mixture all at once. Mix lightly until just combined, taking care not to overmix.

Spoon mixture into prepared pans. Sprinkle tops of muffins with pinenuts.

Bake for 20 to 25 minutes, until a skewer inserted in the center of a muffin tests clean.

Cool in pan for 5 minutes, then transfer to a wire rack. Serve warm, or reheat gently just before serving.

SUN-DRIED TOMATO MUFFINS

Makes 12

2 ¼ cups (185g) all-purpose (plain) flour

2 ¼ tsp baking powder

1 small onion, finely chopped

½ tsp salt

¼ tsp chili powder

1 cup (125g) grated cheddar

1 egg, beaten

¼ cup (60ml) olive oil

2 Tbsp tomato paste

1 ¼ cups (310ml) milk

½ cup (25g) chopped sun-dried tomatoes

Preheat oven to 375ºF (190ºC). Grease a standard muffin pan or line with paper liners.

Sift flour and baking powder into a large mixing bowl. Add onion, salt, chili and grated cheese, and toss well to combine.

Whisk egg, oil, tomato paste and milk together in another bowl. Stir in sun-dried tomatoes

Make a well in the dry ingredients. Pour egg mixture into the well. Stir just enough to form a batter, taking care not to overmix.

Spoon the mixture into prepared muffin pan. Bake for 25 minutes, until firm and golden brown.

Cool in pan for 5 minutes, then transfer to a wire rack. Serve muffins warm or at room temperature.

CHEESE & CARROT MUFFINS

Makes 12

3 cups (375g) all-purpose (plain) flour

3 tsp baking powder

½ tsp salt

pinch of chili powder

1 cup (125g) grated cheese (cheddar, Swiss, or another of your choice)

2 large carrots, peeled and grated

1 small onion, very finely chopped

1 tsp chopped parsley

1½ cups (375ml) milk

3 Tbsp olive oil

2 eggs, beaten

Preheat oven to 400°F (200°C). Grease a standard muffin pan or line with paper liners.

Sift flour and baking powder into a large mixing bowl. Add salt, chili powder, cheese, carrot, onion and parsley and toss well to combine. Make a well in the center.

Mix together milk, oil and eggs and pour into the well. Stir just enough to combine.

Spoon into prepared pan. Bake for 25 to 30 minutes, until puffed and golden brown.

Cool in pan for 5 minutes, then transfer to a wire rack to cool completely.

BUTTERMILK, CHEESE & BACON MUFFINS

Makes 12

2 cups (250g) all-purpose (plain) flour

2 tsp baking powder

1 cup (80g) grated parmesan

½ cup (80g) chopped cooked bacon

4 tsp snipped chives

⅔ cup (160ml) buttermilk

1 stick (125g) butter, melted

1 egg, lightly beaten

4oz (100g) camembert, cut into 12 pieces

Preheat oven to 350°F (180°C). Lightly grease a standard muffin pan.

Sift flour and baking powder into a large mixing bowl. Stir in parmesan, bacon and chives. Make a well in center of dry ingredients.

Combine buttermilk, butter and egg. Mix into dry ingredients, until just combined.

Spoon into the prepared pan to one-third full. Add a piece of camembert to each muffin and top evenly with the remaining mixture.

Bake for 25 to 30 minutes, until the center of a muffin springs back when pressed.

Cool in pan for 5 minutes, then transfer to a wire rack. Serve warm, or reheat gently before serving.

DOUBLE CORN MUFFINS

Makes 6

1 ½ cups (190g) all-purpose (plain) flour

1 ½ tsp baking powder

1 cup (160g) medium cornmeal (polenta)

½ cup (65g) grated cheddar or Swiss cheese

1 ¼ cups (310ml) milk

2 eggs

6 ½ Tbsp (100g) butter, melted and cooled

1 cup (165g) canned corn kernels in brine, drained

Preheat oven to 400ºF (200ºC). Lightly grease a Texas muffin pan.

Sift flour and baking powder into a large mixing bowl. Stir in cornmeal and cheese. Make a well in center of dry ingredients.

Whisk together milk, eggs and butter. Pour into dry ingredients and stir gently to combine. Fold in corn.

Spoon mixture into prepared pan. Bake for 25 minutes, until golden and springy to the touch.

Cool in pan for 5 minutes. Serve muffins while still hot or gently reheat before serving.

Muffin note Double corn muffins are ideal made fresh for breakfast, served with bacon and roasted tomatoes.

SPICY SALAMI MUFFINS

Makes 12

2 cups (250g) all-purpose (plain) flour

2 tsp baking powder

1 cup (160g) finely diced salami

1 cup (125g) grated parmesan

½ cup (80g) pitted olives, chopped

⅓ cup (10g) chopped parsley

1 tsp chili flakes

1 Tbsp milk

6 Tbsp (90g) butter, melted

1 egg, lightly beaten

Preheat oven to 350°F (180°C). Lightly grease a standard muffin pan.

Sift flour and baking powder into a large bowl. Stir in salami, parmesan, olives, parsley and chilli.

Combine milk, butter and egg. Make a well in the center of the dry ingredients. Add milk mixture all at once. Mix lightly, until just combined.

Spoon mixture evenly into prepared pan.

Bake for 20 to 25 minutes, until a skewer inserted in the center of a muffin tests clean. Cool in pan 5 minutes, then transfer to a wire rack to cool completely.

MINI HERB MUFFINS WITH SMOKED SALMON

Makes 36

2 ½ cups (315g) all-purpose (plain) flour

3 tsp baking powder

½ tsp salt

1 cup (125g) grated Swiss cheese

1 onion, finely diced

¼ cup (10g) chopped fresh herbs, such as parsley, basil or dill

2 eggs, beaten

2 Tbsp olive oil

1 ¼ cups (310ml) milk

¼ cup (35g) grated parmesan cheese, for sprinkling

3 ½ oz (100g) sliced smoked salmon, for filling

½ cup (115g) sour cream, for filling

basil leaves, for filling

Preheat oven to 400°F (200°C). Grease three mini muffin pans.

Sift the flour, baking powder and salt into a large mixing bowl. Add cheese, onion and herbs and mix well, then make a well in the center.

Add the eggs, oil and milk to the well. Stir to just combine, taking care not to overmix.

Spoon mixture into prepared pans and sprinkle each muffin with some parmesan.

Bake for 10 to 15 minutes, until puffed and golden brown. Cool in pan for 5 minutes, then transfer to a wire rack to cool completely.

No more than 1 hour before serving, split muffins and fill with a piece of smoked salmon and a little sour cream. Garnish each with a small basil leaf. Keep cool until serving.

BRIE & CHARGRILLED PEPPER MUFFINS

Makes 12

2 cups (250g) all-purpose (plain) flour

2 tsp baking powder

1/3 cup (45g) chopped chargrilled red pepper (capsicum)

1/4 cup (30g) pinenuts

1 tsp salt

4 tsp chopped parsley

2/3 cup (160ml) milk

1 stick (125g) butter, melted

1 egg, lightly beaten

2oz (60g) brie, cut into 12 cubes

Preheat oven to 350°F (180°C). Lightly grease a standard muffin pan.

Sift flour and baking powder into a large bowl. Stir in red pepper, pinenuts, salt and parsley.

Whisk together milk, butter and egg.

Make a well in the dry ingredients. Add milk mixture and stir until just combined, taking care not to overmix.

Half fill recesses in prepared pan with muffin batter. Top each with a cube of brie. Cover evenly with remaining muffin mixture.

Bake for 20 to 25 minutes, until the top of a muffin springs back when pressed.

Cool in pan for 5 minutes, then transfer to a wire rack. Serve warm, or reheat gently before serving.

BARBEQUE BEEF & FETA MUFFINS

Makes 6

2 cups (250g) all-purpose (plain) flour

2 tsp baking powder

1 cup (250ml) milk

2 eggs, lightly beaten

½ cup (125ml) olive oil

½ cup (65g) grated cheddar

Barbeque beef filling

1 Tbsp olive oil

5oz (140g) ground beef (mince)

¼ cup (60ml) barbeque sauce

¼ cup (15g) sliced sun-dried tomatoes

2oz (60g) feta, crumbled

tomato ketchup, for serving

Preheat oven to 400°F (200°C). Lightly grease a Texas muffin pan and line with jumbo paper liners.

To make barbeque beef filling, heat oil in large skillet (fry-pan) on high. Add beef, brown well for 4 to 5 minutes, breaking up clumps with a wooden spoon as it cooks. Stir barbeque sauce, tomato and feta into beef. Remove from heat and set aside to cool slightly.

To make muffins, sift flour and baking powder together into a large mixing bowl. Make a well in center.

Whisk together milk, eggs and oil, and pour these into the well. Stir until just combined.

Spoon mixture into prepared liners to half full. Add a heaped tablespoon of barbeque beef filling. Spoon over remaining batter to cover filling. Sprinkle with cheddar.

Bake for 15 to 20 minutes, until golden brown. Serve warm with tomato ketchup.

CHEESY HAM & PINEAPPLE MUFFINS

Makes 12

2 ½ cups (315g) all-purpose (plain) flour

4 tsp baking powder

1 tsp salt

7oz (200g) ham, diced

1 Tbsp superfine (caster) sugar

1 cup (125g) grated sharp cheese, such as cheddar

⅓ cup (10g) snipped chives

1 ¼ cups (310ml) milk

1 egg

4 Tbsp (60g) butter, melted

14oz (400g) canned crushed pineapple, drained

Preheat oven to 350°F (180°C). Line two Texas muffin pans with jumbo paper liners.

Sift flour, baking powder and salt together into a large bowl. Add ham and sugar, and half the cheese and half the chives, reserving the remaining cheese and chives in a bowl. Toss well to combine.

Whisk milk, egg and butter together.

Make a well in the dry ingredients. Pour milk mixture into well, add pineapple, and gently mix into flour mixture until just combined.

Spoon mixture evenly into prepared liners to two-thirds full. Bake for 20 minutes, until lightly golden and the center of a muffin springs back when pressed.

Sprinkle the tops of muffins with remaining cheese and chives. Return to oven for 4 to 5 minutes, until cheese melts.

Cool in pan for 5 minutes, then transfer to a wire rack. Serve warm, or reheat gently before serving.

CHILI SPINACH MUFFINS

Makes 12

3 cups (375g) all-purpose (plain) flour

3 tsp baking powder

1 cup (30g) firmly packed, finely shredded spinach

1 small onion, finely diced

½ tsp salt

½ tsp chili powder

1 egg, beaten

3 Tbsp Thai sweet chili sauce

½ cup (125ml) olive oil

1½ cups (375ml) milk

3 Tbsp sesame seeds

Preheat oven to 375°F (190°C). Grease a standard muffin pan or line with paper liners.

Sift flour and baking powder into a large mixing bowl. Add the spinach, onion, salt and chili powder, and toss well to combine. Make a well in the center.

In another bowl, mix together egg, chili sauce, oil and milk.

Pour wet ingredients into the well in the dry ingredients and stir to combine, taking care not to overmix.

Spoon mixture into prepared pan. Sprinkle top of muffins with sesame seeds.

Bake for 25 minutes, until a skewer inserted in the center of a muffin tests clean.

Cool in pan for 5 minutes, then transfer to a wire rack to cool completely.

SPICY VEGETABLE MUFFINS

Makes 10

1 ½ cups (190g) all-purpose (plain) flour

3 tsp baking powder

¼ tsp chili powder

½ tsp salt

3 small eggs, lightly beaten

2 Tbsp olive oil

¾ cup (180ml) milk

14oz (400g) canned corn (kernels), drained

1 small onion, finely diced

1 small red bell pepper (capsicum), deseeded and finely diced

3 Tbsp snipped chives

Preheat oven to 400°F (200°C). Lightly grease 10 recesses in a standard muffin pan with oil.

Sift flour, baking powder, chili powder and salt into a bowl and make a well in the center.

Place eggs, oil, milk, corn, onion, red pepper and chives in a bowl and stir to combine.

Pour wet mixture into the well and stir briefly to just combine.

Spoon mixture into prepared pan and bake for 20 minutes, or until the top of a muffin springs back when lightly pressed.

Cool in pan for 5 minutes, then tramsfer to a wire rack to cool completely.

CUPCAKES & MUFFINS FOR CHILDREN

CUPCAKE STUDIO

Children love to decorate cupcakes.
This is a fun activity for a party.
Arrange a workstation at the right
height, with cooled cupcakes (prepare
several batches, if you need to),
several bowls of different frostings
and lots of decorations. Then, let the
fun begin!

Makes 12

1 stick (125g) butter, softened

¾ cup (170g) superfine (caster) sugar

1 tsp vanilla extract

2 eggs

1 ½ cups (190g) all-purpose (plain) flour

1 ½ tsp baking powder

½ cup (125ml) milk

Frostings

1 stick (125g) butter, softened

1 ½ cups (225g) confectioners' (icing) sugar

2 Tbsp milk

a few different food colorings and/or ½ tsp finely grated citrus zest, or 1 Tbsp unsweetened cocoa powder

decorations, such as candy balls, sugared shapes, sprinkles (nonpareils), cachous, colored sanding sugar and colored shredded coconut (tinted using a drop of food coloring in ¼ cup (25g) coconut, shaken in a jar)

Preheat oven to 350ºF (180ºC). Line a standard muffin pan with paper cupcake liners.

Using electric mixer, beat butter until fluffy. Add sugar and vanilla essence, and beat until light and fluffy. Add eggs one at a time, beating well after each addition.

In another bowl, sift the flour and baking powder. Fold into the butter mixture, alternating with milk.

Spoon mixture into prepared liners. Bake for 10 to 15 minutes, until a skewer inserted in the center of a cupcake tests clean.

Transfer to a wire rack, and cool completely.

To make frostings, using an electric mixer, beat butter until creamy. Gradually beat in half the confectioners' sugar and all the milk. Beat in remaining confectioners' sugar.

Divide frosting among several bowls. Tint each with a few drops of a different food coloring. Add citrus zest to one color, if you like, or, instead of using food coloring, beat cocoa into one bowl of frosting.

Place each type of decoration in a separate bowl. Make sure there are plenty of small table knives or spoons for children to use when decorating cupcakes.

FAIRY CUPCAKES

Makes 12

1 stick (125g) butter, softened

²/₃ cup (150g) superfine (caster) sugar

1 tsp vanilla extract

2 eggs

1 ¾ cups (220g) all-purpose (plain) flour

1 ¾ tsp baking powder

²/₃ cup (160ml) milk

½ cup (125ml) cream, whipped

multicolored sprinkles (nonpareils), for decorating

Pink glacé frosting

¾ cup (115g) confectioners' (icing) sugar

1 tsp soft butter

a few drops pink food coloring

about 2 tsp boiling water

Preheat oven to 350°F (180°C). Line a standard muffin pan with paper cupcake liners.

Using electric beater, beat butter and sugar together until fluffy. Beat in vanilla. Add eggs one at a time, beating well after each addition.

Sift flour and baking powder into another bowl. Fold flour mixture into butter mixture, alternating with milk, and beginning and ending with flour.

Spoon mixture into prepared liners to two-thirds full. Bake for 20 to 25 minutes, until a skewer inserted in the center of a cupcake tests clean.

Cool in pan for 5 minutes, then transfer to a wire rack to cool completely.

To make pink glacé frosting, sift the confectioners' sugar into a bowl. Beat in butter, food coloring and enough water to make a smooth, spreadable consistency.

Within 1 hour of serving, use a small sharp knife to cut out a small circle from the top of each cupcake. Fill with 1 teaspoon of cream.

Spread top of removed circles with frosting and scatter sprinkles over frosting. Replace circles on top of cream.

PEANUT BUTTER CUPCAKES

Makes 18

1 ¼ cups (160g) all-purpose (plain) flour

¾ cup (170g) light brown (soft brown) sugar

1 ½ tsp baking powder

¾ cup (190ml) milk

⅓ cup (100g) smooth peanut butter

1 egg

2 Tbsp rice bran oil or peanut oil

½ cup (95g) semisweet (plain) chocolate, chopped

Peanut butter frosting

½ cup (150g) smooth peanut butter

4 Tbsp (60g) butter, softened

1 cup (150g) confectioners' (icing) sugar, sifted

1 Tbsp milk

Preheat oven to 400°F (200°C). Line a standard muffin pan with paper cupcake liners.

Place flour, sugar, baking powder, milk, peanut butter, egg, oil and chocolate in a food processor and pulse for 10 to 20 seconds, until combined. Scrape sides and base of bowl with a spatula and pulse again until smooth.

Spoon into prepared liners. Bake for 20 minutes, until a skewer inserted in the center of a cupcake tests clean.

Remove from pan and cool on a wire rack.

To make peanut butter frosting, use electric mixer to beat peanut butter and butter until smooth. Beat in confectioners' sugar and milk. Spread over cooled cupcakes.

PURPLE CHOCOLATE MUFFINS

Makes 12

1 ¾ cups (220g) all-purpose (plain) flour

1 ¾ tsp baking powder

½ cup (110g) superfine (caster) sugar

8oz (225g) canned beets in their juice

7oz (200g) semisweet (plain) chocolate, chopped

1 stick (125g) butter, chopped

2 eggs, lightly beaten

Preheat oven to 400°F (200°C). Line a standard muffin pan with paper liners.

Whisk together flour, baking powder and sugar in a large bowl.

Drain beets, reserving juice. Mash beets or pulse in food processor.

Place chocolate and butter in a heatproof bowl and place over a pan of simmering water on low heat. Stir until melted and smooth.

Add chocolate mixture and mashed beets to dry ingredients, then add reserved beet juice and egg. Stir until just combined.

Spoon mixture into prepared liners. Bake for 15 to 20 minutes, until a skewer inserted in the center of a muffin tests clean.

Cool in pan for 5 minutes, then transfer to a wire rack to cool completely.

Muffin note It can be difficult to convince children to eat enough vegetables. This recipe is a great way to sneak a little extra vegetable content into your little ones' diet!

BUTTERFLY CAKES

Makes 12

1 stick (125g) butter, softened

¾ cup (170g) superfine (caster) sugar

1 tsp vanilla extract

2 eggs

1²/₃ cups (210g) all-purpose (plain) flour

1²/₃ tsp baking powder

½ cup (125ml) milk

1¼ cups (310ml) cream, whippped

confectioners' (icing) sugar, for dusting

Preheat oven to 350ºF (180ºC). Line a standard muffin pan with paper cupcake liners.

Using electric mixer, beat butter and sugar until fluffy. Beat in vanilla, then add the eggs one at a time, beating well after each addition.

Sift flour and baking powder into another bowl. Fold into butter mixture, alternating with milk, and beginning and ending with the flour mixture.

Spoon mixture evenly into prepared liners to two-thirds full. Bake for 15 to 20 minutes, until a skewer inserted in the center of a cupcake tests clean.

Cool in pan for 5 minutes, then transfer to a wire rack to cool completely.

When ready to serve, use the tip of a knife to cut a deep circle from the top of each cake. Pile whipped cream into the top of each cake. Cut reserved circles in half and position in cream to resemble wings. Dust with confectioners' sugar.

CHOCOLATE BUTTERFLY CAKES

Makes 12

1 stick (125g) butter, softened

¾ cup (170g) superfine (caster) sugar

2 eggs

1¼ cups (160g) all-purpose (plain) flour

¼ cup (30g) unsweetened cocoa powder

1¼ tsp baking powder

½ cup (125ml) milk

¼ cup (85g) strawberry jelly (jam)

1 cup (250ml) cream, whipped, for decorating

multicolored sprinkles (nonpareils), for decorating

confectioners' (icing) sugar, for dusting

Preheat oven to 350°F (180°C). Line a standard muffin pan with paper cupcake liners.

Using electric mixer, beat butter and sugar until fluffy. Add eggs one at a time, beating well after each addition.

Sift flour, cocoa and baking powder into another bowl. Add flour mixture to butter mixture, alternating with milk.

Spoon the mixture evenly into prepared liners. Bake for 15 to 20 minutes, until a skewer inserted in the center of a cupcake tests clean. Transfer to a wire rack to cool.

When ready to serve, use the tip of a knife to cut a deep circle from the top of each cake. Spoon a little jelly into each hole in the top of each cake. Pile whipped cream on top of the jelly.

Cut reserved circles in half and position in cream to resemble butterfly wings. Decorate with sprinkles and dust with confectioners' sugar.

STRAWBERRIES & CREAM CUPCAKES

Makes 12

1 stick (125g) unsalted butter, softened

⅔ cup (150g) superfine (caster) sugar

2 eggs

1 tsp vanilla extract

1¼ cups (160g) all-purpose (plain) flour

1¼ tsp baking powder

½ cup (125ml) milk

1¼ cups (310ml) cream, whipped

9oz (250g) strawberries, hulled and halved

confectioners' (icing) sugar, for dusting

Preheat oven to 350°F (180°C). Line a standard muffin pan with paper cupcake liners.

Using electric mixer, beat butter and sugar in a large bowl until fluffy. Add eggs, one at a time, beating well after each addition. Add vanilla extract and mix gently to combine.

Sift flour and baking powder into a small bowl. Fold flour mixture and milk alternately into butter mixture, beginning and ending with flour.

Fill prepared liners and bake for 15 to 20 minutes, until a skewer inserted in the center of a cupcake tests clean. Transfer to a wire rack to cool.

When ready to serve, spoon or pipe whipped cream onto each cupcake and top with halved strawberries. Dust with confectioners' sugar.

PEAR & CINNAMON MUFFINS

Makes 18

2 cups (250g) all-purpose (plain) flour

1 Tbsp baking soda (bicarbonate of soda)

1 ½ tsp ground cinnamon, + extra, for dusting

½ cup (110g) superfine (caster) sugar

2 eggs, lightly beaten

1 cup (250ml) milk

⅔ cup (160ml) light olive oil

2 ripe pears, peeled, cored, diced

Preheat oven to 400°F (200°C). Lightly grease 18 recesses in two standard muffin pans.

Whisk together flour, baking soda, cinnamon and sugar in a large mixing bowl.

Combine egg, milk and oil, then stir into the dry ingredients until just combined. Gently fold in two-thirds of pear.

Spoon into prepared pans and top each muffin with remaining pear. Dust with extra cinnamon and bake for 20 minutes, until golden and the center of a muffin springs back when pressed.

Cool in pan for 5 minutes, then transfer to a wire rack to cool completely.

OAT & DATE MUFFINS

Makes 12

2 cups (250g) all-purpose (plain) flour

2 ½ tsp baking powder

½ cup (45g) old-fashioned rolled oats + ¼ cup (20g) extra

½ cup (80g) chopped pitted dates

½ cup (110g) raw (turbinado) sugar

¼ cup (15g) wheat bran

finely grated zest of 1 orange

1 stick (125g) butter, melted

⅓ cup (80ml) milk

⅓ cup (80ml) fresh orange juice

1 egg, lightly beaten

Preheat oven to 350°F (180°C). Lightly grease a standard muffin pan.

Sift flour and baking powder together into a large bowl. Stir in oats, dates, sugar, bran and orange zest. Make a well in center of dry ingredients.

Combine butter, milk, orange juice and egg. Pour into well of dry ingredients and lightly mix, until just combined.

Spoon mixture into prepared pan to three-fourths full. Sprinkle extra oats on top of muffins.

Bake for 15 to 20 minutes, until a skewer inserted in the center of a muffin tests clean.

Cool in pan for 5 minutes, then transfer to a wire rack to cool completely.

PAINTBOX CUPCAKES

Makes 16

2 sticks (250g) butter, softened

1 cup (225g) superfine (caster) sugar

3 eggs

1 tsp vanilla extract

2 ¼ cups (280g) all-purpose (plain) flour

2 ¼ tsp baking powder

¾ cup (190ml) milk

3 Tbsp unsweetened cocoa powder

1 Tbsp milk, extra

a few drops pink or blue food coloring

multicolored sprinkles (nonpareils), for decorating

Buttercream frosting

1 stick + 2 Tbsp (150g) butter, softened

2 cups (300g) confectioners' (icing) sugar

2 Tbsp milk

a few drops pink food coloring

Preheat oven to 350°F (180°C). Line 16 recesses of two standard muffin pans with paper cupcake liners.

Using electric mixer, beat butter and sugar together until fluffy. Add eggs, one at a time, beating well after each addition. Beat in vanilla.

In another bowl, sift flour and baking powder. Lightly fold flour mixture into creamed mixture, alternating with milk.

Divide mixture into three portions in separate bowls. Leave one portion plain. Make a paste using cocoa powder and extra milk, and add to another portion. Add a few drops of food coloring to the third portion.

Drop heaped teaspoons of each color into each prepared liner to two-thirds full. Swirl batter gently with a skewer to combine colors slightly.

Bake 20 to 25 minutes, until a skewer inserted in the center of a cupcake tests clean. Cool in pan for 5 minutes, then transfer to a wire rack to cool completely.

To make buttercream frosting, beat butter with an electric mixer until fluffy. Add confectioners' sugar and milk, beating well until thick and light. Beat in a few drops of coloring. Spread over cooled cupcakes. Decorate with sprinkles.

PRETTY IN PINK CUPCAKES

Makes 12

1 ½ cups (190g) all-purpose (plain) flour

1 ½ tsp baking powder

1 stick (125g) butter, softened

¾ cup (170g) superfine (caster) sugar

2 eggs, lightly beaten

½ cup (125ml) milk

1 tsp vanilla extract

pink sprinkles (nonpareils), for decorating

Pink frosting

1 ½ cups (225g) confectioners' (icing) sugar, sifted

2 Tbsp (30g) butter, melted

2 drops red food coloring

1 Tbsp boiling water

Preheat oven to 350°F (180°C). Line a standard muffin pan with paper cupcake liners.

Sift flour and baking powder into a large mixing bowl and add butter, sugar, egg, milk and vanilla. Using an electric mixer on low speed, beat until combined. Beat for 1 minute more, until mixture is pale and smooth.

Spoon mixture into prepared liners. Bake for 15 to 20 minutes, until a skewer inserted in the center of a cupcake tests clean. Transfer to a wire rack to cool.

To make pink frosting, beat all the ingredients together until smooth. Spread over cooled cupcakes and decorate with sprinkles.

BLUEBERRY BRAN MUFFINS

Makes 12

¼ cup (60ml) rice bran oil or other vegetable oil

3 Tbsp light corn syrup

1 Tbsp molasses

¼ cup (55g) superfine (caster) sugar

2 eggs

1 cup (250ml) milk

1½ cups (60g) wheat bran flakes

1 cup (125g) all-purpose (plain) flour

1 tsp baking powder

1 tsp pumpkin pie spice (mixed spice)

1 cup (125g) fresh or frozen blueberries

Preheat oven to 350°F (180°C), and grease a standard muffin pan.

Place oil, corn syrup, molasses, sugar, eggs and milk in a bowl, then beat just to combine.

Whisk together the wheat bran flakes, flour, baking powder and spice in a large mixing bowl. Make a well in the center. Pour the wet ingredients into the well and stir to combine, then gently stir in the blueberries.

Spoon mixture into prepared pan. Bake for 25 minutes, until a skewer inserted in the center of a muffin tests clean.

Cool in pan for 5 minutes, then transfer to a wire rack to cool completely.

CHEESE & HAM MEGA MUFFINS

Makes 6

2 cups (250g) all-purpose (plain) flour

2 tsp baking powder

¼ tsp salt

1 cup (125g) grated cheddar

½ cup (80g) chopped ham

⅓ cup (50g) chopped sun-dried tomatoes

3 Tbsp chopped parsley

1 cup (250ml) milk

¼ cup (60ml) olive oil

1 egg, beaten

Preheat oven to 350°F (180°C). Lightly grease a Texas muffin pan.

Sift flour, baking powder and salt into a large mixing bowl. Add three-fourths of the cheese and all the ham, tomatoes and parsley. Toss well to combine.

Whisk together milk, oil and egg. Make a well in center of flour mixture and stir in milk mixture, until just combined, taking care not to overmix.

Spoon mixture evenly into prepared pans. Sprinkle remaining cheese on top.

Bake for 20 minutes, until a skewer inserted in the center of a muffin tests clean. Serve warm or at room temperature.

ROCKY ROAD CUPCAKES

Makes 12

1 stick (125g) butter, softened

²/₃ cup (150g) light brown (soft brown) sugar

2 eggs

¾ cup (95g) all-purpose (plain) flour

¼ cup (30g) unsweetened cocoa powder

1 ¼ tsp baking powder

⅓ cup (80ml) milk

¾ cup (70g) unsweetened fine desiccated coconut

Rocky road topping

5oz (150g) semisweet (plain) chocolate, chopped

¼ cup (60ml) cream

18 pink and white marshmallows, halved

⅓ cup (30g) unsweetened shredded (desiccated) coconut, toasted

¼ cup (35g) natural peanuts, chopped

¼ cup (40g) candied (glacé) cherries, chopped

Preheat oven to 350ºF (180ºC). Line a standard muffin pan with paper cupcake liners.

Using electric mixer, beat butter and sugar together until fluffy. Add eggs one at a time, beating well after each addition.

Sift flour, cocoa and baking powder together. Lightly fold into butter mixture, alternating with milk and beginning and ending with flour. Fold in coconut.

Spoon mixture into prepared liners to two-thirds full.

Bake for 20 to 25 minutes, until a skewer inserted in the center of a cupcake tests clean. Cool in pan for 5 minutes. Transfer to a wire rack to cool completely.

To make rocky road topping, combine chocolate and cream in a saucepan. Heat on low, stirring constantly, until smooth. Set aside for 10 minutes, until slightly thickened. Spread generously on the cooled cupcakes. Top with the marshmallows, shredded coconut, peanuts and cherries, pressing gently into the chocolate to set.

FINANCIER CAKES

WHAT ARE FINANCIERS?

Financiers are little French cakes made to an unusual recipe, which has a very simple method. Confectioners' (icing) sugar is mixed with almond meal and often also flour. Next, a little melted butter is added, along with egg whites which have been beaten only until loose bubbles form. This constitutes the basic recipe for financier cakes. But, just like cupcakes and muffins, endless variations are possible.

Originally, they were always made in small rectangular pans, but these days they are most often found baked in an oval shape, in multi-cake pans that have recesses with a ⅓ cup (85ml) capacity. The rectangular

shape is thought to have been used because the French pastry chef who created financiers had a shop close to the Paris stock exchange, and the shape resembled gold bars.

It is also fine to bake financiers in standard muffin pans, or mini loaf pans (which are usually larger then the other types of pans mentioned). They can also be baked in mini muffin pans.

Over the last 10 years or so, financiers have become extremely popular in many countries. They are also often called friands, a term which derives from 'friandise', meaning 'sweet'.

Financiers are ideal tea cakes, make a good school lunch treat, and are also very good dessert cakes, served with whipped cream and fruit.

Eat financiers quickly!
Because of their low fat content, financiers are best eaten on the day they are baked.

Serve financiers while they are still a little warm, or at room temperature. Store in an airtight container once they are cool, but avoid refrigeration.

Freeze them
Financiers can also be individually wrapped in plastic wrap, then sealed in an airtight container and frozen for up to two months. Then defrost in the refrigerator or at room temperature. Only dust with confectioners' sugar or cocoa powder after defrosting.

All those yolks
Making financiers results in leftover egg yolks. Store leftover egg yolks in an airtight container in the fridge for up to 3 days, and use them to bind meatloaf or meatballs, make mayonnaise, enrich pastry or make hollandaise sauce for eggs benedict.

BERRY FINANCIERS | Gluten-free

Makes 12

1 ½ cups (225g) confectioners' (icing) sugar

½ cup (80g) rice flour

1 cup (120g) almond meal

6 egg whites

1 tsp vanilla extract

1 ¼ sticks (155g) butter, melted

1 cup (125g) fresh berries, such as blackberries, raspberries or sliced strawberries

Preheat oven to 400°F (200°C). Grease a 12-recess oval financier pan.

Sift sugar and rice flour into a large mixing bowl. Add almond meal and stir to combine.

In another bowl, whisk egg whites until frothy. Add whites to dry ingredients with vanilla and butter, then stir briefly to just combine.

Spoon mixture evenly into prepared pan to two-thirds full. Top each friand with some berries, pressing them in lightly.

Bake for 20 to 25 minutes, until golden brown and springy to the touch.

Stand financiers in the pan for 5 minutes, then transfer to a wire rack to cool.

WHITE CHOCOLATE, PISTACHIO & HAZELNUT FINANCIERS

Makes 8

1 ½ cups (225g) confectioners' (icing) sugar

½ cup (65g) all-purpose (plain) flour

1 cup (120g) hazelnut meal

½ cup (65g) chopped shelled natural pistachios

¾ cup (145g) white chocolate morsels (chips)

6 egg whites

1 ½ sticks (185g) butter, melted

extra confectioners' (icing) sugar, for dusting

Preheat oven to 350°F (180°C). Lightly grease eight recesses of a mini loaf pan.

Sift sugar and flour together into a large mixing bowl. Mix in hazelnut meal, pistachios and half of the chocolate.

In another bowl, lightly whisk egg whites until frothy. Add to dry ingredients and mix lightly. Stir in butter, until combined.

Spoon mixture into prepared pan. Sprinkle each cake with remaining chocolate.

Bake for 15 to 20 minutes, until golden and a skewer inserted in the center of a cake tests clean.

Cool in pan for 5 minutes, then transfer to a wire rack to cool completely.

Financier note Instead of a mini loaf pan, you can use a standard muffin pan or oval financier cake pan. In this case, the recipe will make 12 cakes.

LIME & COCONUT FINANCIERS

Makes 12

1 ½ cups (225g) confectioners' (icing) sugar

½ cup (65g) all-purpose (plain) flour

1 cup (120g) almond meal

¼ cup (25g) unsweetened fine desiccated coconut

2 tsp finely grated lime zest

6 egg whites

1 ½ sticks (185g) butter, melted

3 Tbsp fresh lime juice

⅓ cup (30g) unsweetened coconut flakes

Preheat oven to 375°F (190°C). Grease a 12-recess oval financier pan.

Sift sugar and flour into a large mixing bowl. Add almond meal, coconut and lime zest and stir to combine.

In another bowl, whisk egg whites until frothy. Stir into dry ingredients, then add butter and lime juice and stir to combine.

Spoon mixture evenly into prepared pan. Sprinkle cakes with coconut flakes.

Bake for about 20 minutes, until a skewer inserted in the center of a cake tests clean. Stand in pan for 5 minutes, then transfer to a wire rack to cool.

MINI CHERRY FINANCIERS

Makes 36

1 ½ cups (225g) confectioners' (icing) sugar

½ cup (65g) all-purpose (plain) flour

1 cup (120g) almond meal

1 ½ sticks (185g) butter, melted

6 egg whites

7oz (200g) fresh or frozen pitted cherries

Preheat oven to 375°F (190°C). Grease three mini muffin pans.

Sift the sugar and flour into a large mixing bowl. Stir in the almond meal.

In another bowl, whisk egg whites until frothy. Add whites and butter to dry ingredients and stir until just combined.

Spoon level tablespoons of mixture into prepared pans. Press a cherry into each cake.

Bake for about 15 minutes, until lightly browned and springy to the touch. Stand in pans 5 minutes, then transfer to a wire to cool.

PEACH FINANCIERS

Makes 12

1 ½ cups (225g) confectioners' (icing) sugar

½ cup (65g) all-purpose (plain) flour

1 cup (120g) almond meal

1 ½ sticks (185g) butter, melted

6 egg whites

14oz (400g) canned peach slices, drained, chopped

extra confectioners' (icing) sugar, for dusting

Preheat oven to 350ºF (180ºC). Lightly grease a 12-recess oval financier pan or standard muffin pan.

Sift the sugar and flour into a large mixing bowl. Mix in the almond meal.

Make a well in the center of the dry ingredients and mix in butter, stirring gently, until just combined.

In another bowl, lightly whisk egg whites until frothy. Stir egg white into almond mixture. Lightly stir in three-fourths of the chopped peach.

Spoon mixture evenly into prepared pan. Top each cake with some of the reserved peach.

Bake for 20 to 25 minutes, until a skewer inserted in the center of a cake tests clean.

Cool in pan for 5 minutes, then transfer to a wire rack to cool. Dust with confectioners' sugar just before serving.

APRICOT & LEMON FINANCIERS

Makes 12

1 ½ cups (225g) confectioners' (icing) sugar

½ cup (65g) all-purpose (plain) flour

1 cup (120g) almond meal

¾ cup (120g) dried apricots, chopped + 1 Tbsp extra

finely grated zest of 1 lemon

6 egg whites

1 ½ sticks (185g) butter, melted

1 Tbsp fresh lemon juice

Preheat oven to 350°F (180°C). Lightly grease a 12-recess oval financier pan.

Sift confectioners' sugar and flour into a large mixing bowl. Mix in almond meal, dried apricots and zest.

In another bowl, lightly whisk egg whites until frothy. Add to dry ingredients and mix lightly. Mix in butter and lemon juice until combined.

Spoon mixture into prepared pan. Sprinkle each financier with extra dried apricots.

Bake for 15 to 20 minutes, until golden and a skewer inserted in the center of a cake tests clean.

Cool in pan for 5 minutes, then transfer to a wire rack to cool completely.

PECAN & RASPBERRY HAZELNUT FINANCIERS

Makes 8

1¼ cups (190g) confectioners' (icing) sugar

²/₃ cup (90g) all-purpose (plain) flour

1 cup (120g) hazelnut meal

5 egg whites

1½ sticks (185g) butter, melted

½ cup (65g) fresh or frozen raspberries

8 pecans

extra confectioners' (icing) sugar, for dusting

Preheat oven to 400°F (200°C). Grease eight recesses in a mini loaf pan.

Sift the sugar and flour into a large mixing bowl. Mix in the hazelnut meal.

Lightly whisk egg whites until frothy. Add to dry ingredients and mix lightly. Add butter, stirring until combined.

Spoon mixture evenly into prepared pan. Top each cake with a few raspberries and a pecan.

Bake for 15 to 20 minutes, until golden and firm.

Cool in pan for 5 minutes, then transfer to wire rack to cool. Dust with confectioners' sugar before serving.

SPICED PEAR & COCONUT FINANCIERS

Makes 12

1 ½ cups (225g) confectioners' (icing) sugar, sifted

½ cup (65g) all-purpose (plain) flour, sifted

1 Tbsp ground cinnamon

1 cup (90g) unsweetened fine desiccated coconut

6 egg whites

1 stick + 3 Tbsp (170g) butter, melted and cooled

1 firm, ripe pear, cored, finely sliced

Preheat oven to 400°F (200°C). Grease a 12-recess oval financier pan or standard muffin pan.

Whisk together confectioners' sugar, flour, cinnamon and coconut in a bowl.

In another bowl, whisk egg whites until frothy. Make a well in the center of dry ingredients, then pour in egg whites and melted butter. Stir briefly to just combine.

Spoon mixture into prepared pan, filling only to two-thirds full. Top each cake with some pear slices.

Bake for 25 minutes, until golden brown and a skewer inserted in the center of a cake tests clean. Cool in pan for 5 minutes, then transfer to a wire rack to cool.

PRALINE CHOCOLATE & STRAWBERRY FINANCIERS

Makes 12

1 ¼ cups (190g) confectioners' (icing) sugar

⅔ cup (90g) all-purpose (plain) flour

1 cup (120g) almond meal

5 egg whites

1 ½ sticks (185g) butter, melted

4oz (100g) praline chocolate bar, chopped

3 strawberries, hulled, sliced

Preheat oven to 400°F (200°C). Lightly grease a 12-recess oval financier pan.

Sift sugar and flour into a large mixing bowl, and whisk in the almond meal.

In another bowl, whisk egg whites until frothy. Mix egg whites, then butter, into dry ingredients, stirring until combined. Fold chocolate into mixture.

Spoon mixture into the prepared pan. Top each cake with a strawberry slice, pressing in gently.

Bake for 20 to 25 minutes, until golden and firm.

Cool in pan for 5 minutes, then transfer to a wire rack to cool.

RASPBERRY BREAKFAST FINANCIERS

Makes 8

1¼ cups (190g) confectioners' (icing) sugar

⅔ cup (90g) all-purpose (plain) flour

1 cup (120g) almond meal

5 egg whites

1½ sticks (185g) butter, melted

½ cup (65g) fresh or frozen raspberries

¼ cup (25g) old-fashioned rolled oats

extra confectioners' (icing) sugar, for dusting

Preheat oven to 400°F (200°C). Grease eight recesses in a mini loaf pan.

Sift sugar and flour into a large mixing bowl. Add almond meal and stir to combine.

In another bowl, whisk egg whites until frothy. Stir into dry ingredients. Stir in melted butter, until combined.

Spoon mixture evenly into prepared pan. Top the cakes with raspberries, pressing in gently. Sprinkle evenly with the rolled oats.

Bake for 15 to 20 minutes, until golden and firm.

Cool in pan for 5 minutes, then transfer to a wire rack to cool. Dust with confectioners' sugar.

APPLE PECAN FINANCIERS

Makes 8

1⅓ cups (200g) confectioners' (icing) sugar

⅔ cup (90g) all-purpose (plain) flour

1 cup (120g) almond meal

5 egg whites

1 tsp vanilla extract

1½ sticks (185g) butter, melted

1 green apple, peeled, cored, finely chopped

½ cup (75g) pecans

extra confectioners' (icing) sugar, for dusting

Preheat oven to 400°F (200°C). Grease eight recesses in a 12-recess oval financier pan.

Sift the sugar and flour into a large mixing bowl. Whisk in the almond meal.

Very lightly mix the egg whites and vanilla, using a fork. Add to the dry ingredients, then mix lightly. Pour in the melted butter, then stir until well combined. Fold in the apple.

Spoon the mixture into the prepared pan to two-thirds full. Decorate the tops of the cakes with pecans.

Bake for 15 minutes, or until golden and firm to the touch.

Cool in pan for 5 minutes, then transfer to a wire rack to cool. Dust with confectioners' sugar before serving.

CHOCOLATE & MACADAMIA FINANCIERS

Makes 8

1½ cups (225g) confectioners' (icing) sugar, sifted

1 cup (120g) almond meal

½ cup (65g) all-purpose (plain) flour

¼ cup (30g) unsweetened cocoa powder, sifted

6 egg whites

1½ sticks (185g) butter, melted

½ cup (65g) roughly chopped macadamias

extra confectioners' (icing) sugar, for dusting

Preheat oven to 400°F (200°C). Grease eight recesses in a 12-recess oval financier pan.

Whisk together confectioners' sugar, almond meal, flour and cocoa powder in a large mixing bowl.

In another bowl, whisk egg whites until frothy. Fold into dry ingredients with melted butter, mixing until just combined.

Spoon into prepared pan. Sprinkle macadamias over cakes.

Bake for 20 to 25 minutes, until a skewer inserted in the center of a cake tests clean. Cool in pan for 5 minutes, then transfer to a wire rack to cool. Dust with confectioners' sugar before serving.

MANGO & COCONUT FINANCIERS

Makes 12

6 egg whites

3 small mangoes, cheeks removed, peeled

1 cup (120g) almond meal

1 ½ cups (225g) confectioners' (icing) sugar, sifted

½ cup (65g) all-purpose (plain) flour, sifted

1 ½ sticks (185g) butter, melted

¼ cup (25g) unsweetened shredded (desiccated) coconut

confectioners' (icing) sugar, for dusting

Preheat oven to 375°F (190°C). Lightly grease a 12-recess oval financier pan.

In a large bowl, lightly whisk egg whites until frothy.

Reserve 1 mango cheek and dice the others. Gently mix diced mango, almond meal, sugar and flour into egg white. Stir in butter gently.

Spoon mixture into prepared pan to two-thirds full. Thinly slice reserved mango, crosswise. Top each cake with a mango slice and sprinkle with shredded coconut.

Bake for 20 to 25 minutes, until center of a cake springs back when pressed.

Cool in pan for 5 minutes, then transfer to a wire rack to cool. Dust with confectioners' sugar before serving.

SPECIAL
OCCASIONS

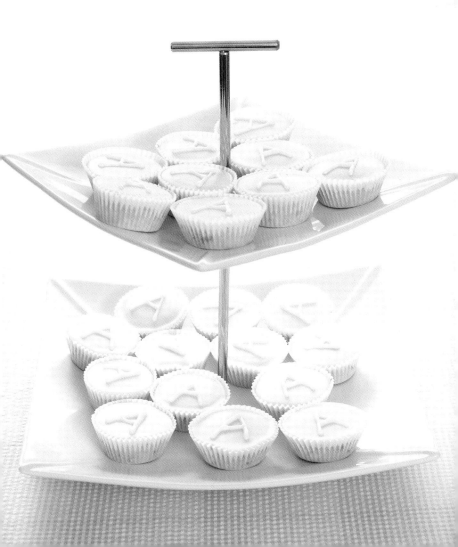

CELEBRATION MENU IDEAS

Bridal shower

Have servers pass trays of each item (allow one of each per guest) during the party, to be enjoyed with sparkling wine.

- Mini Herb Muffins with Smoked Salmon (page 192)
- small savory tartlets
- squares of frittata
- simple vegetable hors d'oeuvres such as asparagus wrapped with ham

Then present a platter of cakes (allow 2 cakes per person) and serve several varieties of tea.

- Cherry and Coconut Cupcakes (page 36)
- Mini Orange Cupcakes (page 74)
- Mini Cherry Financiers (page 244)
- Coconut Meringue Cupcakes (page 28)

Relaxed birthday brunch

Arrange everything in the center of the table or on a buffet, so your guests can help themselves.

- juices
- sliced fresh fruit
- homemade bakery basket:
  Mixed Berry Oat Muffins (page 154)
  Applesauce Muesli Muffins (page 146)
  Buttermilk, Cheese & Bacon Muffins (page 186)
- coffee and tea

GET DECORATING

While a light dusting of cocoa powder or confectioners' (icing) sugar is often all the decoration needed for little cakes, on special occasions, it's worth taking the time and effort to create something truly spectacular.

There are many different types of sprinkles and decorations available for decorating little cakes. Here are some popular choices.

Colored gels

Sprinkles (jimmies/nonpareils)

Sugar pearls

Silver dragees and gold dragees

Colored sanding sugar

Edible gold leaf and silver leaf

Edible glitter

Molded sugar or marzipan decorations

Gum paste flowers and gum paste cut-outs

Fondant cut-outs and fondant shapes

Piped melted chocolate

Frosting

There are many types of frosting, and many ways to vary them such as by adding flavorings (vanilla extract, citrus zest, cocoa) and color. In this book, you will find recipes for cream cheese frosting, confectioners' (icing) sugar-based frosting, buttercream frosting and ganache (a delicious, rich combination of chocolate and cream).

When making confectioners' sugar-based frostings or chocolate ganache, alter the consistency to change the decorative effect. Keep the consistency thick for sculpted or piped frosting which will stay in place. Make the consistency thinner for overflowing drips and glaze-like effects.

Frosting should be fun. Don't be afraid to try using a piping bag; the more often you do, the more skilled you will become. You can start by using a plain nozzle, and gradually work your way up to using a star nozzle and creating

elegant swirls. Remember, any imperfections will still taste great!

If you are decorating cakes for an important occasion, try to make time for at least one practice session.

If you are very unsure, you can still make beautiful cupcakes by applying frosting with a small palette knife. Or, if that is still too daunting, use readymade Royal frosting. Roll it out to ⅛ inch (3mm) thick, and use an appropriately sized round cutter to cut circles from the frosting.

Brush the top of the cupcakes with melted apricot jelly (jam) and gently press the frosting on top. Royal frosting can be decorated by creating patterns in the rolled-out frosting before cutting it into circles. Try pressing the back of a knife blade into the frosting to make a diamond quilting pattern.

HOW TO MAKE A CUPCAKE WEDDING CAKE

Make a tiered stand in the same way as for Tiers of Flower Cupcakes, page 294. Instead of arranging cupcakes on the top tier, it is usual to make one larger cake for this tier, for the traditional cake-cutting ceremony. Make the cake in a size to fit the top tier, either using the same recipe as for the cupcakes, or using a cake recipe of your choice. Frost this cake to match the cupcakes.

When it comes to decorating the cupcakes, don't be too ambitious. Here are some simple hints to help you achieve a great result.

Customize the frosting colors to match the overall theme and decor of the wedding.

Use a piping bag fitted with a star-shaped nozzle to apply large mounds of frosting to each cake. Stack the cakes on your cupcake stand, alternating the colors. This is an elegant way to display your wedding cupcakes with a minimum of work.

If you can't pipe swirls, then choose a flat frosting. See Rose Petal Cupcakes, page 298, for a simple, effective style of cupcake decoration, suitable for a wedding.

Make use of bought decorations such as ribbons, lace, edible glitter, dragees and even sugared almonds.

Use fresh flowers or artificial flowers. If fresh, make sure you choose something non-toxic with a mild fragrance that doesn't overpower the flavor of the cakes. Edible flowers are best, such as mini roses, rose petals or pansies. Buy florists' tape to wrap the cut stems, which you can cover with satin ribbon fixed with a tiny pin.

You don't need an enormous tiered stand if you have many guests. Make up extra cupcakes and decorate in the same way, but keep these aside for serving on trays.

Packed in individual boxes, with matching ribbons, cupcakes make ideal wedding favors.

BABY CAKES

Makes 36

3 sticks (375g) butter, softened

2 cups (550g) superfine (caster) sugar

3 tsp vanilla extract

6 eggs

4 ¼ cups (530g) all-purpose (plain) flour

4 ¼ tsp baking powder

2 cups (500ml) milk

1 Tbsp multicolored sprinkles (nonpareils)

Frosting

3 cups (450g) confectioners' (icing) sugar, sifted

2 Tbsp butter, softened

⅓ cup (85ml) milk

green and pink food coloring

readymade white glossy decorating gel or frosting, for decorating

Preheat oven to 350°F (180°C). Line three standard muffin pans with white paper cupcake liners.

Using electric mixer, beat butter, sugar and vanilla in a very large mixing bowl until fluffy. Beat in eggs, one at a time.

Sift flour and baking powder together and add to butter mixture, alternating with milk, stirring to combine. Fold in multicolored sprinkles.

Spoon mixture into prepared liners to three-fourths full. Bake for 20 to 25 minutes, until a skewer inserted in the center of a cupcake tests clean. If your oven will not acccommodate all the pans on the same rack, swap the pans from higher to lower positions after 10 minutes, to ensure even cooking.

Transfer to a wire rack to cool.

To make frosting, combine confectioners' sugar, butter and milk in a medium heatproof bowl.

Place bowl over a small pan of simmering water. Whisk over heat until mixture has a smooth, spreadable consistency. Remove half the frosting to a separate bowl. Tint one half pale green, using a drop of food coloring at a time until the desired depth of color is achieved. Tint the other half using pink food coloring.

Spoon pale green frosting over half the cakes, leaving the bowl over hot water as you work. Stand cupcakes on a wire rack until the frosting sets.

Spoon pink frosting over remaining cakes; stand until frosting sets.

Decorate cakes by piping the initial of the baby's name on top of each cake, using decorating gel.

Cupcake note Plain, unfrosted cakes can be frozen in a sealed container for up to one month. Defrost the cakes at room temperature before decorating.

Frosted cakes can be prepared up to a day in advance. Store them in an airtight container at room temperature overnight.

CARROT TOP CUPCAKES

Makes 12

1 ½ cups (190g) all-purpose (plain) flour

½ cup (110g) superfine (caster) sugar

1 tsp baking powder

¾ tsp baking soda (bicarbonate of soda)

½ tsp salt

1 cup (110g) grated raw carrot

½ cup (125g) undrained, canned crushed pineapple

2 eggs, lightly beaten

¾ cup (190ml) vegetable oil

½ tsp vanilla extract

½ cup (65g) chopped walnuts

Cream cheese frosting

½ cup (75g) confectioners' (icing) sugar

2oz (60g) cream cheese, softened

grated zest of 1 orange or lemon

Marzipan carrots

7oz (200g) readymade marzipan

orange food coloring

12 sprigs of dill

Preheat oven to 350ºF (180ºC). Line a standard muffin pan with paper cupcake liners.

Sift flour, sugar, baking powder, baking soda and salt together into a large mixing bowl. Add carrot, pineapple, egg, oil and vanilla and stir until combined. Stir in walnuts.

Spoon into prepared pan. Bake for 25 minutes, until a skewer inserted in the center of a cupcake tests clean. Transfer cupcakes to wire racks to cool.

To make cream cheese frosting, beat sugar into cream cheese until mixture is light and fluffy. Add grated zest, to taste. Spread generously over cooled cupcakes.

To make marzipan carrots, knead enough orange food coloring into marzipan to match the color of carrots. Break off walnut-sized pieces of the orange marzipan and roll into carrot shapes. Using a non-serrated knife, score the surface to make creases in the carrots. Make a hole in the end of the carrot with a toothpick and push in a sprig of dill.

Press a carrot onto each frosted cake.

EASTER BUNNY CUPCAKES

Makes 10

½ cup (125ml) hot water

1 cup (225g) superfine (caster) sugar

1 stick (125g) butter, chopped

4oz (100g) semisweet (plain) chocolate, chopped

2 Tbsp milk

1 cup (125g) all-purpose (plain) flour

2 Tbsp unsweetened cocoa powder

1 tsp baking powder

1 egg, lightly beaten

Buttercream frosting

1 stick (125g) butter, softened

1½ cups (225g) confectioners' (icing) sugar

2 Tbsp milk

¼ cup (25g) unsweetened fine desiccated coconut

Bunny faces

thin licorice straps

20 pieces small white oval candy

20 blue and 10 brown mini candy-coated chocolate balls

10 pink marshmallows, cut in half

Preheat oven to 350ºF (180ºC). Line 10 recesses in a standard muffin pan with paper cupcake liners.

Combine water, sugar, butter, chocolate and milk in a medium saucepan. Stir over low heat until smooth. Transfer mixture to a medium bowl. Cool for 10 minutes.

Sift flour, cocoa powder and baking powder into another bowl. Fold flour mixture and egg into cooled chocolate mixture, mixing just to combine.

Spoon mixture evenly into prepared liners, filling nearly to the top.

Bake for 20 to 25 minutes, until a skewer inserted in the center of a cake tests clean.

Cool in pan for 5 minutes, then transfer to a wire rack to cool completely.

To make buttercream, use electric mixer to beat butter until very pale. Gradually beat in sugar and milk in two batches. Spread over cooled cupcakes.

To make bunny faces, sprinkle frosting with coconut. Decorate with licorice for mouth and whiskers, white candy for teeth, mini candy balls for eyes and nose, and marshmallow for ears.

HOT CROSS MUFFINS

Makes 8

2 cups (250g) all-purpose (plain) flour

½ cup (110g) superfine (caster) sugar

2 tsp baking powder

2 tsp pumpkin pie spice (mixed spice)

½ cup (80g) currants

2 Tbsp chopped mixed peel

2 eggs, lightly beaten

½ cup (125ml) liquid honey

1 stick (125g) butter, melted

1 tsp vanilla extract

1 cup (250ml) natural unsweetened yogurt

4oz (100g) white chocolate, melted, for decorating

Preheat oven to 400ºF (200ºC). Line eight recesses in a standard muffin pan with paper liners.

Sift flour, sugar, baking powder and spice into a large bowl. Stir in currants and peel. Make a well in the center.

Place the eggs, honey, butter, vanilla and yogurt in another bowl and whisk to combine. Pour the wet ingredients into the well in the center of the dry ingredients and stir just enough to combine.

Spoon mixture into prepared liners and bake for 20 minutes, until the center of a muffin springs back when pressed.

Transfer to a wire rack to cool completely.

Decorate muffins by piping a cross of melted white chocolate over the surface.

MINI EASTER EGG FINANCIER CAKES

Makes 8

1 cup (150g) confectioners' (icing) sugar, sifted

⅔ cup (80g) almond meal

½ cup (65g) all-purpose (plain) flour, sifted

3 Tbsp unsweetened cocoa powder

⅓ cup (80ml) canola or light olive oil

⅓ cup (80ml) milk

3 egg whites

8 mini chocolate candy Easter eggs, halved

extra unsweetened cocoa powder, for dusting

Preheat oven to 350ºF (180ºC). Lightly grease eight recesses in an oval financier pan.

Whisk together sugar, almond meal, flour and cocoa powder in a large mixing bowl. Make a well in the center.

Pour oil and milk into well and stir until smooth.

In another bowl, lightly whisk egg whites until frothy. Stir into batter, until just combined.

Spoon evenly into prepared pan. Top each cake with two Easter egg halves.

Bake for 12 to 15 minutes, until a skewer inserted in the center of a cake tests clean.

Cool in pan for 10 minutes, then transfer to a wire rack to cool completely. Dust with cocoa before serving.

FATHER'S DAY GOLF CUPCAKES

Makes 12

1 stick (125g) butter, softened

2/3 cup (100g) superfine (caster) sugar

2 eggs

grated zest of 2 limes

1 tsp coconut extract

1 1/4 cups (160g) all-purpose (plain) flour

1 1/4 tsp baking powder

1/3 cup (80ml) milk

3/4 cup (70g) unsweetened fine desiccated coconut + extra 1/3 cup (30g), for decorating

few drops green food coloring, for decorating

12 paper flags, for decorating

12 dry tapioca pearls, for decorating

Cream cheese frosting

3oz (90g) cream cheese, at room temperature

2 Tbsp (30g) unsalted butter, softened

1 tsp coconut extract

1 1/2 cups (225g) confectioners' (icing) sugar

Preheat oven to 350°F (180°C). Line a standard muffin pan with paper cupcake liners.

Using electric mixer, beat butter and sugar together until fluffy. Add eggs one at time, beating well after each addition. Beat in zest and extract.

Sift flour and baking powder into another bowl. Fold flour mixture into butter mixture, alternating with milk. Fold in 3/4 cup (70g) coconut.

Spoon mixture into prepared liners to two-thirds full. Bake for 20 to 25 minutes, until a skewer inserted in the center of a cupcake tests clean.

Cool in pan for 5 minutes, then transfer to a wire rack to cool completely.

To make cream cheese frosting, use an electric mixer to beat cream cheese, butter and extract together until creamy. Gradually beat in the confectioners' sugar, until smooth. Spread over cooled cupcakes.

Combine extra coconut and green food coloring in small sealed plastic bag. Close bag, shake a few times and then, using fingers, rub coconut from outside of bag until green in color. Sprinkle cupcakes with green coconut, then decorate each with a paper flag and one tapioca pearl for the golf ball.

MYSTERY CAKES

They look sweet, but they taste savory…
mysterious.

Makes 12

14oz (400g) zucchini (courgette), coarsely
grated

3 slices of bacon, finely chopped

1 large onion, finely chopped

1 cup (125g) all-purpose (plain) flour

1 tsp baking powder

½ tsp salt

5 eggs, lightly beaten

1 cup (120g) grated Swiss cheese

¼ cup (60ml) rice bran oil or peanut oil

slices of raw carrot, for decorating

slices of cucumber skin, for decorating

Cream cheese frosting

9oz (250g) cream cheese, at room
temperature

3 Tbsp milk

Preheat oven to 400°F (200°C). Lightly grease a standard muffin pan.

Stir together all the cake ingredients in a bowl. Spoon into prepared pan.

Bake for 20 minutes, until a skewer inserted in the center of a cake tests clean. Stand in pan for 5 minutes, then transfer to a wire rack to cool completely.

To make cream cheese frosting, beat cream cheese and milk. Spread generously over cooled cupcakes

Use Halloween shaped cutters such as ghosts and bats to cut decorations from carrot and cucumber slices. Press carrot and cucumber shapes onto frosting.

SCARY CHOCOLATE CUPCAKES

Makes 12

1 stick (125g) butter, softened

1 cup (225g) superfine (caster) sugar

1 tsp vanilla extract

2 eggs

1⅓ cups (170g) all-purpose (plain) flour

½ cup (55g) unsweetened cocoa powder

1½ tsp baking powder

⅔ cup (160ml) milk

readymade black decorating gel or frosting

6 large chocolate-nut candy balls

24 red mini candy-coated chocolate balls

Buttercream frosting

1 stick (125g) butter, softened

1½ cups (225g) confectioners' (icing) sugar

3 Tbsp milk

3 drops orange food coloring

Preheat oven to 350°F (180°C). Line a standard muffin pan with orange paper cupcake liners.

Using electric mixer, beat butter and sugar until fluffy. Beat in vanilla. Add eggs, one at a time, beating well after each addition.

Sift flour, cocoa powder and baking powder into another bowl. Fold flour mixture into butter mixture, alternating with milk, and beginning and ending with flour.

Spoon mixture into prepared pan and bake for 25 minutes, until a skewer inserted in the center of a cupcake tests clean. Transfer to a wire rack to cool.

To make buttercream frosting, use an electric mixer to beat butter until pale. Beat in half of the sugar, the milk, then the remaining sugar. Mix in coloring. Spread over cupcakes.

To decorate with spiders, pipe black gel to make legs, add half a chocolate ball as the body, then use gel and red balls to make eyes.

THANKSGIVING CAKES

Makes 12

1 ½ cups (225g) confectioners' (icing) sugar

½ cup (65g) all-purpose (plain) flour

1 cup (125g) toasted pecans, finely chopped

¾ cup (120g) dried cranberries

6 egg whites

1 ½ sticks (185g) unsalted butter, melted

extra confectioners' (icing) sugar, for dusting

Preheat oven to 350°F (180°C). Lightly grease a 12-recess oval financier pan.

Sift sugar and flour into a large mixing bowl. Mix in pecans and ½ cup (80g) cranberries.

In another bowl, whisk egg whites until frothy. Add to dry ingredients and mix lightly. Stir in butter just until combined.

Spoon mixture into prepared pan. Sprinkle cakes with remaining cranberries.

Bake for 15 to 20 minutes, until golden and a skewer inserted in the center of a cake tests clean.

Cool in pan for 5 minutes, then transfer to a wire rack to cool. Serve warm, dusted with confectioners' sugar.

HOLLY CUPCAKES

Makes 12

1 stick (125g) butter, softened

¾ cup (170g) superfine (caster) sugar

2 eggs

1 tsp vanilla extract

½ cup (95g) semisweet (plain) chocolate morsels (chips)

2 cups (250g) all-purpose (plain) flour

2 tsp baking powder

⅓ cup (80ml) milk

3½ oz (100g) readymade marzipan

red and green food coloring

White glacé frosting
1½ cups (225g) confectioners' (icing) sugar, sifted

about Tbsp boiling water

2 Tbsp (30g) butter

Preheat oven to 375°F (190°C). Line a standard muffin pan with paper cupcake liners.

Using electric mixer, beat butter and sugar together until fluffy. Add eggs, one at a time, beating well after each addition. Add vanilla and chocolate and stir to combine.

Sift flour and baking powder into another bowl. Lightly fold flour mixture and milk into butter mixture.

Spoon into prepared pan to three-fourths full. Bake for 12 to 15 minutes, until a skewer inserted in the center of a cupcake tests clean.

Cool in pan for 5 minutes, then transfer to a wire rack to cool.

Color three-fourths of marzipan green and remaining fourth red. Roll green to an ⅛ inch (3mm) thickness. Cut out holly leaves, marking veins with the tip of a sharp knife. Roll red marzipan into balls for berries.

To make white glacé frosting, place confectioners' sugar in a bowl. Make a well in center and stir in water and butter, until smooth. Spread on cupcakes. Decorate with marzipan leaves and berries.

CHRISTMAS MINI MUFFINS

Makes 44

1 1/3 cups (170g) all-purpose (plain) flour

1 1/2 tsp baking powder

1/3 cup (75g) dark brown (demerara) sugar

1 egg, lightly beaten

1/2 cup (125ml) rice bran oil or other vegetable oil

1/3 cup (80ml) milk

1 1/2 cups (240g) readymade Christmas fruit mince

decorative holly sprigs

Preheat oven to 400°F (200°C). Place mini paper cupcake liners into four mini muffin pans.

Sift the flour and baking powder into a large mixing bowl and mix in the sugar.

In another bowl, combine egg, oil, milk and fruit mince. Fold into the dry ingredients.

Spoon just under 1 tablespoon of mixture into each paper liner (you may not use all of them). Bake for 15 minutes, until well risen and golden.

Transfer to a wire rack. Top each muffin with a decorative holly sprig. Serve warm or at room temperature.

TIERS OF FLOWER CUPCAKES

Makes 40

4 sticks (500g) unsalted butter, chopped

11oz (300g) white chocolate, chopped

4 cups (900g) superfine (caster) sugar

2 cups (500ml) milk

4 cups (500g) all-purpose (plain) flour

1 tsp baking powder

2 tsp vanilla extract

4 eggs

Frosting

1 cup (250ml) double (heavy) cream

1lb 5oz (600g) white chocolate, chopped

Preheat oven to 325ºF (160ºC). Grease 40 recesses in four standard muffin pans.

Combine butter, chocolate, sugar and milk in a large saucepan. Stir over low heat, until chocolate has melted and sugar has dissolved. Transfer the mixture to a large bowl; cool to room temperature.

Stir in sifted flour and baking powder, the vanilla and the eggs, mixing well.

Spoon mixture into prepared pans to three-fourths full.

Bake for 20 minutes, until a skewer inserted in the center of a cupcake tests clean.

Stand cakes in pans for 5 minutes, then carefully transfer to a wire rack to cool completely.

To make frosting, bring cream to a boil in a saucepan. Pour cream over chocolate in a large bowl, stir until chocolate has melted.

Cover mixture and refrigerate, stirring occasionally, for about 30 minutes, or until the mixture thickens to a spreadable consistency. Using a small palette knife, evenly spread the tops of the cupcakes with frosting.

Cupcake note If your oven can only take two pans at a time, make all the cupcake batter at once, but cook in two batches, using only two pans each time.

Cupcake stand and decorations

craft glue

12 x 5 inch (12cm) clear plastic pillars

1 each of 6 inch (15cm), 8 inch (20cm), 10 inch (25cm), 12 inch (30cm) and 14 inch (35cm) round silver-covered cake boards

40 white paper cupcake liners

43 assorted colored miniature gerberas (or flowers of your choice)

florists' tape

For the stand, glue three of the pillars in a triangular shape around the center of the largest cake board (use the picture for reference). Glue the next size down of the cake boards on top.

Repeat, glueing pillars and stacking boards of decreasing size. Allow glue to set overnight. Place each frosted cupcake into a paper cupcake liner.

Trim stalks from 40 of the flowers and bind cut ends with florists' tape. Position a flower on top of each cupcake, in the center.

 Arrange cupcakes on the stand. Use the remaining flowers to decorate the top of the stand, taping their stems together, and placing them in the gap at the center of the cupcakes.

Flower note Make sure that the flowers you use have not been sprayed with chemicals and avoid those with a strong perfume. Explain to your florist that they will be placed on frosting.

FROSTED CHOCOLATE CUPCAKE BIRTHDAY CAKE

Makes 15

1 stick (125g) butter, softened

1½ cups (335g) superfine (caster) sugar

1 tsp vanilla extract

2 eggs

1½ cups (190g) all-purpose (plain) flour

1½ tsp baking powder

¼ cup (30g) unsweetened cocoa powder

1 cup (250ml) milk

Rich chocolate frosting
1 cup (250ml) double (heavy) cream

13oz (370g) semisweet (plain) chocolate morsels (chips)

Preheat oven to 400°F (200°C). Line 15 recesses in two standard muffin pans with paper cupcake liners.

Using an electric mixer, beat butter, sugar and vanilla until fluffy. Beat in eggs, one at a time.

Sift together flour, baking powder and cocoa powder and add to butter mixture in three batches, alternating with milk, and beating well after each addition.

Spoon into prepared paper liners and bake for 15 minutes, until a skewer inserted in the center of a cupcake tests clean. Transfer to a wire rack to cool.

To make rich chocolate frosting, place cream and chocolate in a bowl and melt over a saucepan of simmering water. Stir until smooth, then set aside to cool. Beat frosting with an electric mixer until creamy.

Pipe frosting onto cooled cupcakes and arrange on a tiered plate to serve.

ROSE PETAL CUPCAKES

Makes 12

12 cupcakes, not frosted or decorated (try Raspberry and Lemon Cupcakes, page 42, or Coconut Cupcakes, page 70)

Frosted rose petals
1 egg white

12 edible rose petals (must not have been sprayed)

¼ cup (55g) superfine (caster) sugar

Rose frosting
1½ cups (225g) confectioners' (icing) sugar, sifted

about 3 tsp rosewater

1 Tbsp boiling water

pink food coloring

To make frosted rose petals, whisk egg white until foamy and brush onto rose petals. Place petals on paper towel and dust well with sugar.

Set aside to dry (in the sun, if possible). Store in a single layer on a paper towel, in an airtight container.

To make rose frosting, combine sugar with rosewater and water. Stir until smooth and shiny. Mix in one drop of coloring at a time to make frosting pastel pink.

Spread frosting over cooled cupcakes and, before frosting sets, decorate with frosted rose petals.

GLOSSARY

Ovens

• Cupcakes, muffins and financier cakes can be baked in most types of domestic oven. Just preheat the oven to the recipe's recommended temperature, which is given in degrees Farenheit and then degrees Celsius (ie) 350°F (180°C).

Temperatures

°F	°C	Gas mark
225	110	¼
250	120/130	½
275	140	1
300	150	2
325	160/170	3
350	180	4
375	190	5
400	200	6
425	220	7
450	230	8
475	240	9

Weights and measurements

• Most home cooks find it easiest to measure ingredients by using measuring cups and measuring spoons, so these recipes have been written to suit that approach.

In this book:
1 tsp (1 teaspoon) = 5 ml
1 Tbsp (1 tablespoon) = 15 ml
1 cup = 250ml
and
2 Tbsp is very close to 1 fluid ounce
2 cups is very close to 1 pint

Exact definitions of these measurements may vary very slightly from one country to another, but don't worry about that when using this book. The tiny differences will not affect these recipes.

Converting volume to weight

Each ingredient has a different mass, so it must be weighed out separately to convert the volume measurement to a weight measurement. Here are a few useful volume-to-weight guidelines.

    1 tsp baking powder = 0.15oz (4.5g)
    1 tsp baking soda = 0.15oz (4.5g)
    1 cup flour = 4oz (125g)
    1 cup white sugar = 8oz (225g)
    1 cup brown sugar = 8oz (225g)
    1 cup chocolate morsels = 6oz (190g)

Dairy Products

• **Butter** If the ingredients list calls for 'butter', this means regular salted butter. Some recipes call for 'unsalted butter'. The two butters are interchangeable – just

adjust any salt measurements to suit, by perhaps a very small pinch for every stick (125 g) of butter.

• **Milk** Most of these recipes can be made with the milk of your choice; low fat, regular, soy, etc

• **Cream** Single or pouring cream is suitable to be used as a liquid addition to a mixture. Heavy or double cream must be used for whipping. It is also useful for thick chocolate frostings.

• **Yogurt** For best results, use a low-fat or regular unsweetened yogurt that is neither very thin (liquid) or very thick.

• **Buttermilk** This thick, cultured milk is excellent for baking. It gives a tangy, rich flavour and moist results.

• **Sour cream** This is a richer type of cultured dairy product than buttermilk, and it gives very similar results. It has less moisture content, so is not a good measure-for-measure substitute for milk or buttermilk. Some milk must also be added for such a substitution to give a successful result.

Sugar

There are many types of sugar.

- Sugar (white sugar/granulated white sugar) is the most common sugar used in cooking.
- Superfine sugar (caster sugar) is also a white sugar, with much smaller crystals than granulated white sugar. Bakers often prefer to use superfine sugar because the crystals dissolve into mixtures very easily. Sugar and superfine sugar can easily be used in place of each other.
- Confectioners' sugar (powdered sugar/icing sugar) is very finely ground white sugar that is powdery in texture. It is used in cooking, in frostings (icings), and for dusting cakes and muffins once baked and cooled.
- Light brown sugar (soft brown sugar) contains white sugar and some molasses, which gives some moisture, a brown color and a light molasses flavor.
- Dark brown sugar (demerara sugar) contains more molasses than light brown sugar, so has a stronger color and flavor.
- Raw sugar (turbinado sugar) is produced from the first stage of sugar refinement, and has large granules with a light brown color.
- Sanding sugar is a white sugar with

particularly large crystals, which are sometimes colored. It is used decoratively.

- Vanilla sugar can be bought, or you can make your own by placing a vanilla bean in a jar of white sugar or superfine sugar, and leaving it there for at least a week for the vanilla to perfume the sugar.

- It is usually suitable to use (white) sugar or superfine (caster) sugar in place of light brown (soft brown) sugar, and to use light brown sugar in place of any of these white sugars. However, the color and flavor of the cakes or muffins will change as a result of this substitution, as, sometimes will the texture.

Flours and starches

- All-purpose flour (plain flour/white flour/ cake and cookie flour) is a milled white wheat flour that is used in most cake recipes.

- Whole wheat flour (wholemeal flour) is made from the whole wheat grain; the outer bran, which is the fiber component.

- Rice flour (rice starch) is ground rice. Rice flour is gluten-free so can be used to replace wheat flour for gluten-intolerant people.

- Cornstarch (cornflour) is milled corn (maize). It is a very 'short' starch, which is to say it makes doughs very crumbly.

Nut meals

Add delicious flavor and moist texture to your baking. Cakes that contain nut meal will probably remain light and fresh for an extra day, so consider recipes containing nut meal when you need to do baking in advance. To avoid rancidity, store nut meals in the freezer.

- Almond meal is made by grinding almonds finely. You can make your own using a food processor, but take care to stop grinding the nuts before their oil is released, which makes the meal very sticky and lumpy.
- Hazelnut meal is made by grinding hazelnuts in the same way.

Baking soda (bicarbonate of soda) and baking powder

These are both rising agents which are added to dough or batter.

- Baking soda is pure sodium bicarbonate, and when it is mixed with acidic ingredients ,it releases bubbles of carbon dioxide which expand the mixture. Baking soda reacts immediately, so a recipe that contains it needs to be baked quickly.
- Baking powder contains sodium bicarbonate along with an acidic component, which is usually cream of tartar. It often contains a drying agent, too, which is a starch.
- Avoid substituting one of these for the other; the quantities do not correspond, the flavors are different and the recipe will often work with one but not the other.

Eggs

- Eggs in these recipes are assumed to be chicken's eggs, approximately 1 ¾ oz or 50 to 53g in size. A 'large egg' means an egg of approximately 2oz or 60 to 63g.
- To separate an egg into white and yolk, gently crack the shell against a hard surface, hold the egg over a small bowl, and use the tips of your thumbs to break the shell into two halves. Catch the yolk in one half while the white falls into the bowl below, and release the rest of the white into the bowl by gently tipping the yolk from one half shell to the other. Place the yolk in another bowl. If the yolk breaks into the

white, discard the white, as the yolk will prevent the white from being whipped into a stiff foam.

- To beat whites loosely, use a fork and beat until large bubbles form.
- To beat whites to soft peaks, use a whisk or electric beater fitted with whisks, and beat only until the whites become white and glossy but still have a soft, floppy texture.
- To beat whites to stiff peaks, use a whisk or electric mixer fitted with whisks, and beat until the whites become very white and glossy and have a firm texture, so that if you lift the whisk from the whites, the mixture will stand in stiff peaks. Take care not to overbeat whites past this point, as they will suddenly become crumbly and lumpy, and no longer useable.
- Take care with yolks when adding them to a bowl before mixing. Sugar will 'burn' or 'cook' yolks if left to sit. Only add the sugar to the yolks, or the yolks to the sugar, when you are ready to begin mixing.

Chocolate

Types of chocolate

- Unsweetened chocolate (baker's chocolate, bitter chocolate) is pure cocoa mass (a combination of the fermented cocoa bean's two products, which are cocoa solids and cocoa butter) with no added sugar. It is unpleasant to eat in its uncooked state, but is favored by professional bakers who like to control the exact type and amount of sugar in their baking.
- Bittersweet chocolate (sometimes known as bitter chocolate) has a high cocoa mass content and very little sugar. Most people find this chocolate too bitter to eat. It is suitable, though, for cookery.
- Semisweet chocolate (plain chocolate/dark chocolate) has a fairly high cocoa mass and some sugar content. It is pleasant to eat and particularly good for cookery, delivering rich, dark, chocolatey results.
- Milk chocolate is made with the addition of milk and has a fairly high sugar content. It is very smooth and sweet, and much paler in color than the other chocolates listed above.

- White chocolate is technically not a chocolate at all. It is made from cocoa butter along with sugar and often milk, too. It is very sweet and has a mild caramel flavor.
- Compound chocolate is a mixture of cocoa mass, sugar and various other products, so is considered to be a confectionery product rather than actual chocolate. It is not suitable for most cookery.

Forms of chocolate
- Bars are slabs of chocolate, usually divided into squares to be easily broken apart. Use bars when chopped chocolate is called for.
- Morsels (chips/melts/buttons/drops/callets) are round, evenly sized drops of chocolate ready for melting or adding to cooking.

- Chips. While this term refers to large drops of chocolate in some countries, in this book the term chip means a small rod of chocolate. Chopped chocolate is a suitable substitute.

Storage tips
- Unbaked cupcake, muffin or financier cake batter cannot be frozen or refrigerated.
- Allow cooked items to cool completely before wrapping in plastic wrap or sealing in an airtight container. Or, cooked cakes can be stored at room temperature for 1 to 2 days.
- Refrigerate cooked items for up to a week.
- Individual muffins or financier cakes can be reheated by microwaving for 9 seconds on 75% power, or by placing in a 325°F (160°C) oven for 5 to 10 minutes. Frosted cupcakes should not be reheated.

Cooked cupcakes, muffins and financier cakes can often also be frozen
- Arrange on layers of wax paper, either in a plastic storage box or an airtight bag.
- Defrost in the refrigerator or at room temperature. Then dust with confectioner's sugar or cocoa.
- Frosted cakes cannot be frozen.

INDEX

ACKNOWLEDGMENTS

Recipes and images on pages 26-27, 34-35, 36-37, 50-51 64-65, 68-73, 76-81, 84-87, 104-107, 110-111, 114-115, 118-119, 124-125, 138-139, 146-153, 156-157, 160-163, 182-185, 192-193, 200-201, 214-215, 224-227, 238-239, 252-253, 278-279, 288-289, 296-297 copyright *New Zealand Woman's Weekly*

Images on pages 90-91, 170-171, 271,, 304-305, 310, 313, 317 & 320 copyright *Shutterstock*

All other recipes and images copyright *acpsyndication.com*